Peterson
First Guide
to
Forests

By John Kricher

Illustrated by
Gordon Morrison

D0837340

HOUGHTON MIFFLIN COMPANY
Boston   New York
1994

To Deborah Fahey

Copyright © 1995 by Houghton Mifflin Company
Editor's Note copyright © 1995 by Roger Tory Peterson

PETERSON FIRST GUIDES, PETERSON FIELD GUIDES,
and PETERSON FIELD GUIDE SERIES
are registered trademarks of
Houghton Mifflin Company.

For information about permission to reproduce
selections from this book, write to
Permissions, Houghton Mifflin Company,
215 Park Avenue South, New York, New York 10003

Library of Congress Cataloging-in-Publication Data
Kricher, John C.
Peterson first guide to forests / by John Kricher ;
illustrated by Gordon Morrison.
p.   cm.
Includes index.
ISBN 0-395-71760-4
1. Forest ecology—North America.   2. Forest fauna
—North America—Identification.   3. Forest plants—
North America—Identification.   I. Title.
QH102.K756   1995
574.5'2642'097—dc20   94-23719   CIP

Printed in Italy
NWI 10 9 8 7 6 5 4 3 2 1

Editor's Note

In 1934, my *Field Guide to the Birds* first saw the light of day. This book was designed so that live birds could be readily identified at a distance, by their patterns, shapes, and field marks, without resorting to the technical points specialists use to name species in the hand or in the specimen tray. The book introduced the "Peterson System," as it is now called, a visual system based on patternistic drawings with arrows to pinpoint the key field marks. The system is now used throughout the Peterson Field Guide series, which has grown to over 40 volumes on a wide range of subjects, from ferns to fishes, rocks to stars, animal tracks to edible plants.

Even though Peterson Field Guides are intended for the novice as well as the expert, there are still many beginners who would like something simpler to start with—a smaller guide that would give them confidence. It is for this audience—those who perhaps recognize a crow or a robin, buttercup or daisy, but little else—that the Peterson First Guides have been created. They offer a selection of the animals and plants you are most likely to see during your first forays afield. By narrowing the choices—and using the Peterson System— they make identification even simpler. First Guides make it easy to get started in the field, and easy to graduate to the full-fledged Peterson Field Guides. This one gives the beginner a start on the forests of North America, from the deciduous forests of the eastern United States to the fascinating groves of giant Saguaro in the Southwest.

A forest is much more than its trees. The wildflowers and shrubs, the mammals, the reptiles—and, of course, the birds—that live in the forests combine in different ways to make each one a unique habitat. In the *First Guide to Forests*, John Kricher and Gordon Morrison show you how to tell the forest from the trees. The more you look, the more you will see.

Roger Tory Peterson

Introducing North America's Forests

Much of North America is clothed in wood. In the East, you can hike through lush and varied forest from subtropical Florida to cool, temperate Quebec. In the West, forests of many kinds blanket the various rugged mountain ranges as well as much of the flatter landscape. America's most frequently visited national parks, including Yosemite, Yellowstone, Mt. Rainier, Grand Canyon, Great Smoky Mountains, Shenandoah Valley, Everglades, and Acadia, are located within forests. These forests are far from alike. Some, like the mixed oak and maple forests of the East, are composed mainly of broad-leaved trees whose leaves turn brilliant colors before dropping off in autumn. But many forests, especially those in Canada and the American West, are dominated by needle-leaved trees, the conifers, most of which keep their foliage throughout the year. In some forests, trees such as Redwoods, Common Douglas-firs, Sitka Spruces, and Giant Sequoias grow majestic, well over 200 feet tall, while other forests consist of small, often gnarled junipers and pines that rarely reach 30 feet. Some regions of North America, such as coastal California, for instance, have relatively little forest, with shrubs being the dominant species.

But it takes more than trees to make a forest. Forest habitats consist not only of various species of trees but also of numerous shrubs, wildflowers, ferns, and fungi, all of which taken together support many hundreds of animals, from imposing moose and eagles to humble caterpillars and earthworms and even many forms of life too small to see, such as bacteria. The study of forest natural history is part of the science of ecology, the understanding of how plants and animals interact to form living communities.

Ecology is the scientific study of natural history. It is very satisfying to understand something about what is actually happening in a habitat, in addition to merely knowing, for instance, that those little birds flitting about in the tall Ponderosa Pines are Pygmy Nuthatches. Though nature, at first glance, may look almost hopelessly complex, there are patterns that are not hard to see once you know how to look.

This book will allow you to identify many, if not most, of the common species you are likely to encounter as you travel through North America's varied forests. It is meant to be your introduction to forest ecology. Keep it in your pocket during your travels and use it often.

How to Tell the Forest From the Trees

Each forest type can be recognized by looking for certain indicator species that largely define that forest. Most indicator species are not found in only one kind of forest, so combinations of indicator species are really what define the habitat. For instance, the Black Hills Forest described on page 56 is a unique combination of species, many of which, such as American Elm and Blue Jay, are mainly found in the East and many of which, such as Ponderosa Pine and Lewis's Woodpecker, are fundamentally western in range. It is the combination that is important.

The main focus of this guide is trees, shrubs, wildflowers, birds, mammals, reptiles, and amphibians. Trees are usually the first things you notice about a forest (you can see the forest and the trees!). Shrubs and colorful wildflowers also attract attention. As for animals, although by far the most abundant animals in any forest are insects, spiders, and other invertebrates, most visitors are attracted to the larger creatures, especially birds and mammals.

Opposite each plate is a general description of the forest and brief accounts of how the species illustrated on the plate interact to form the forest community.

It is a good idea to familiarize yourself with all of the plates in the book, because many species occur in more than one major forest type. For instance, the Western Screech-Owl, which is shown in the California Sierra Nevada forest (page 92), is widespread in the West and can be encountered in almost any forest. The more you study the plates, the more you will be able to identify and understand what you see.

Identifying Plants and Animals

Nature is so bountiful that identification can seem downright intimidating at times. However, with a little practice, the task of accurately putting a name on what you are seeing is both fun and satisfying.

Plants: Trees come in two basic kinds, broad-leaved and needle-leaved. Broad-leaved trees such as oaks and maples have wide, flat leaves. Most broad-leaved trees in North America are deciduous, which means they drop their leaves in autumn and grow new leaves in spring. But some broad-leaved species, particularly those in the South, are evergreen and keep their leaves throughout the year.

Broad leaves may be either simple or compound. A simple leaf, like those found on oaks and elms, consists of a single blade on its leafstalk. A compound leaf consists of several leaflets on a single leafstalk. Trees with compound leaves include ashes, locusts, and mesquites. The way leaves are arranged on the stalk is also helpful in identification. Most plants, including wildflowers and shrubs as well as trees, have alternate leaves, but some

NEEDLE-LEAVES   LOBED   COMPOUND

BROAD LEAF   UNLOBED   SIMPLE

Figure 1. Leaf types

have opposite leaves. Leaves may be oval, heart-shaped, pointed, lobed, or elongate. Some leaves have smooth margins, others are toothed. For example, Fremont Cottonwood has broad, heart-shaped leaves with large teeth along the margins, Black Cottonwood leaves are also heart-shaped but have very tiny teeth, and Narrowleaf Cottonwood has elongate leaves with tiny teeth along the margins. The feel of a leaf can also be helpful in identification. Some leaves feel quite waxy and leathery, others are thinner and feel more like paper. Some are covered with fine hairs, usually on their underside.

Needle-leaved trees tend to dominate most cooler forests as well as some very hot and dry forests. Balsam Fir, Ponderosa Pine, Eastern Hemlock, Sitka Spruce, Rocky Mountain Juniper, Baldcypress, and Redwood are all examples of needle-leaved trees. Nearly all are evergreen (the American Larch, or Tamarack, is an exception). Needles may be stiff or soft, long or short. They usually grow in clumps or clusters called bundles, and the number of needles per bundle helps identify the tree. Needle-leaved trees tend to have softer wood than most broad-leaved species.

Needle-leaved trees are conifers, which means that they do not have flowers but produce seeds that are contained in cones. The cones of pines, spruces, hemlocks, and Douglas-firs dangle beneath the branch, but the cones of true firs stand upright. The cones of yews and junipers look like berries.

Broad-leaved trees, shrubs, and wildflowers reproduce by means of flowers. When flowers are present, they are usually very helpful in identifying the plant. Many trees, however, bear small flowers that are hard to see. A hand lens or magnifying glass is quite useful, not only for identification but also for seeing the delicate structures of the flower.

Please keep in mind that many of the most splendid wildflowers are rare, and all are fragile. Treat flowers gently; don't trample them, and avoid picking. A wise conservationist is willing to get down on hands and knees, for the sake of the plant.

Birds: Birding has become a popular pastime because birds are generally conspicuous, both by sight and by sound. Birds tend to be vocal and active during the daylight hours, and many are brightly colored. It's fun to stop at a forest grove and see how many species of birds you can identify. At ground level you may find juncos and thrushes. In the shrubs and low trees might be some chickadees or a small fly-catcher. By craning your neck and peering into the high canopy, you may locate a tanager or some warblers. Some widespread birds of eastern and western forests are shown on pages 14 and 16.

To identify birds, look for field marks, or physical characteristics, such as overall size and shape. Is the bird sparrow-sized, robin-sized, or crow-sized? Note the size and shape of the bill. Is it chunky and thick, like that of a grosbeak, or slender, like that of a warbler or oriole? Note the color and markings. Does the bird have wing bars, wing patches, a white rump, or white outer tail feathers? Does it have an eye ring? Is its breast streaked or spotted?

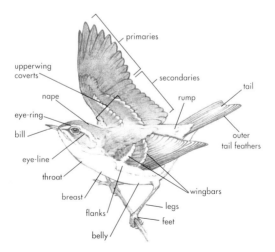

Figure 2. Anatomy of a bird

Behavior also helps with identification. When the bird flies, does it fly straight or tend to undulate? On the ground, does it walk or does it hop? Is it with a flock of others of the same or different species, or is it solitary? What is it eating? How is it feeding, is it on bark or flitting around the outer branches? What is its habitat? Do you find it in a forest, a forest edge, or open brushy field? If in a forest, what kind of forest: pinyon-juniper, open pine, spruce-fir?

Mammals: Mammals generally lack the bright colors of birds, but they are by no means dull. Their coat colors, often subtle in tone, range from pure black or white to many shades of brown, gray, and reddish. Important field marks include overall size and shape, characteristics of the tail (ringed, bushy, naked, short, or long), and the markings on the face.

Many mammal species are most active at dawn or dusk, and some are entirely nocturnal. Many are fairly secretive. Seeing these elusive mammals poses a challenge; many are glimpsed only in the beam of a headlight as they attempt to cross roads at night.

Large mammals like deer, Elk, and bears tend to be easy to identify, but smaller beasts are more challenging. Chipmunks are active during the day and easy to see, but while any chipmunk you see in the east is the Eastern Chipmunk, there are some 20 different species in the West, and they look very much alike.

Reptiles and Amphibians: Reptiles, which have dry, scaly skin, include snakes, lizards, turtles, and alligators. Amphibians, which usually have moist, smooth skin, include salaman-

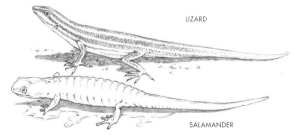

LIZARD

SALAMANDER

Figure 3. Lizard and salamander compared

ders, frogs, and toads. Both reptiles and amphibians are often colorful, but they can nonetheless be very well camouflaged in their environments. Many take refuge beneath rocks and logs, and thus you must search them out.

Amphibians tend to favor wet areas: ponds, streams, swamps, marshes, and wet meadows, though some occur in deserts. Salamanders superficially resemble lizards, but salamanders have moist skin that lacks scales, and their toes are clawless, while lizards have claws and dry, scaly skin.

Search for snakes during the daylight hours by carefully turning over rocks and other debris likely to shelter a resting serpent. (Stand *behind* the rock if you do this—poisonous snakes are common in many areas.) Snakes are best identified by size, color, and pattern. Head shape (slender, wide, triangular) is also helpful in snake identification.

Lizards are frequently seen sunning on rocks. Once warmed, lizards can move very quickly, scampering through dry leaves to shelter. Some lizards can even run on their hind legs for short distances. To identify lizards, note the overall pattern. Some have boldly patterned heads and necks. Note the color and observe whether the scales look smooth or rough. The many kinds of spiny lizards that inhabit the West are, as a group, easily differentiated from the smooth-scaled species.

Forest Types

We have noted that in the East, forests are primarily dominated by deciduous trees, while western forests consist mainly of evergreens. But North America is a huge continent, with countless differences in climate, soils, frequency of natural fires, and other factors. Each subtle difference can result in a different habitat. North America's forests fall into 10 regional groups, which are briefly described here and are illustrated in the pages that follow.

1. Eastern Deciduous Forest. This type occupies nearly all of the eastern United States. It is an immense forest of oaks, hickories, maples, magnolias, elms, sycamores, dogwoods, and other broad-leaved species, though many needle-leaved trees such as Eastern White Pine and Eastern Hemlock also abound. These forests are known for their striking fall colors. Along the sea coast and in the Southeast, deciduous forest gives way to pine forest.

2. Subtropical Evergreen Forest. Most people associate the tropics with equatorial regions, but wet subtropical forest can be found at the southern tip of the Florida peninsula, where mangroves predominate along the coast and mahoganies and palms grow inland, among the grasses of the Everglades.

3. South-Central Texas Forests. Texas is an immense state with an abundance of different kinds of forests. In the area of the Lower Rio Grande River, Texas forests take on the look of subtropical Mexico and include many Mexican species. In south-central Texas, in an area called the Edwards Plateau, a forest of unique junipers supports two endangered bird species as well as more than 400 wildflower species, some of which occur nowhere else.

4. Prairie Riverine Forest. Lush broad-leaved forests line rivers throughout North America, but in dry prairie regions of the central and midwestern states, where grasses and wildflowers dominate, the only areas of forest tend to be along the large rivers and their tributaries. These forests, watered by the rivers, form natural oases for numerous species that otherwise would not occur in the region.

5. Northeastern Boreal Forest. From the north-central and upper New England states north into Canada is a vast forest dominated by conifers, mostly spruces and firs, along with tamaracks, birches, aspens, and various pines. In this region, winters are long and cold, with heavy snowfall, and the summer growing season is only about three months long.

6. Rocky Mountain Forests. The Rockies extend through Canada and eight western states for about 5,000 miles, an immense north-south ridge of rock with peaks routinely exceeding 14,000 feet. Climate changes dramatically with altitude; on a drive of a few hours up a mountain, you can begin on scorching sagebrush desert and end up in a cool spruce-fir forest similar to what you would encounter in Canada. Thus forest habitats change as much with elevation as they do with latitude and longitude. Rocky Mountain forests, as well as those of other western mountain ranges, vary from scrubby, desertlike habitats to tall conifers to timberline forests of stunted, gnarled pines and spruces.

Sometimes the western slopes of mountains are different from the eastern slopes because the mountain range forces moisture-laden air up its western slope, where it condenses and falls as rain. Air that finally reaches the eastern slope is much drier, and the eastern slope is said to be in a rain shadow.

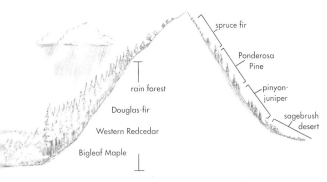

spruce fir

Ponderosa Pine

pinyon-juniper

sagebrush desert

rain forest

Douglas-fir

Western Redcedar

Bigleaf Maple

Figure 4. Rain shadow on eastern slope

7. Southwest Forests. The Southwest is primarily a rugged landscape of hot deserts and grasslands, but the monotonous flatness is broken up periodically by foothill forests of short junipers, oaks, and pines. Many Mexican species occur. Higher mountains support tall pine forest, and at the highest elevations, cool temperatures permit the survival of a mixed forest of spruces, firs, Douglas-fir, and aspens. Down in the desert is one of the most fascinating of all forest habitats, dominated by the magnificent Saguaro, the giant cactus of the Southwest.

8. Sierra Nevada Forests. Extending north-south through much of eastern California, the tall Sierra Nevada range measures 400 miles long and is the home of Yosemite, Kings Canyon, and Sequoia national parks, visited by millions of tourists annually. Like the Rockies, the Sierra Nevada mountains are tall and rugged, with heavy winter snow. Several diverse forest communities are found at different altitudes.

9. California Forests. Even apart from the diverse natural history of the Sierra Nevada range, California, with approximately 800 miles of coastline, is a land of ecological extremes: hot, shrubby deserts such as in Death Valley; cool, foggy groves of statuesque Redwoods along the northern coast; and dry, Mediterranean-type shrublands called chaparral to the south. Approximately 1,500 or 30% of California's plant species occur nowhere else.

10. Pacific Northwest Forests. With an abundance of rain for much of the year, the forests of the Pacific Northwest are uniquely tall and lush. These temperate rain forests include some largely uncut tracts called old-growth forest, which rank among the most magnificent forests in North America. Dense groves of towering Common Douglas-fir, Western Hemlock, and Sitka Spruce are home for such species as the Spotted Owl and Elk.

Some old-growth rain forests are between 500 and 800 years old. These old-growth forests not only provide unique habitat for many species but are themselves imposing examples of nature's artwork. Trees of many ages can be found growing among the stumps and snags of their predecessors, giving the appearance of a forest primeval.

Many old-growth forests are being cut for timber. They are often clear-cut, removing essentially all the trees. Then the area is restocked with trees such as redcedar that grow fast enough to be harvested in less than 100 years. Although the area still produces timber, the diversity and ecological value of old-growth forest is gone. Some tracts of old-growth forest should be conserved for their unique value to wildlife and to human appreciation of nature.

Widespread Birds of Eastern Forests

RED-TAILED HAWK

GREAT HORNED OWL

COMMON FLICKER

male

AMERICAN CROW

RUFFED GROUSE

GREAT CRESTED FLYCATCHER

BROAD-WINGED HAWK

RED-EYED VIREO

OVENBIRD

WOOD THRUSH

Some eastern forest birds are permanent residents; others are present only during the summer breeding season.

RED-TAILED HAWK — 25 in.
A large, bulky, soaring hawk with a white chest and reddish on the upper tail, which is often spread wide when soaring. Permanent resident throughout the West as well.

BROAD-WINGED HAWK — 19 in.
Small, soaring hawk with barred tail, reddish streaks across breast. Summer resident, winters in tropics.

GREAT HORNED OWL — 25 in.
A large, nocturnal owl with distinct feather tufts above each eye. White "bib," heavily barred breast. Call is a resounding *hoot.* Permanent resident, including the West.

AMERICAN CROW — 21 in.
An abundant permanent resident of forests and farmlands throughout most of North America. Gregarious, uniformly black with a purple sheen. Makes a distinctive *caw!*

COMMON FLICKER — 12-14 in.
A brown woodpecker with a spotted breast, often seen on the ground. In flight, shows a conspicuous white rump patch, yellow under wings and tail. Call is a loud *whicka!*

RUFFED GROUSE — 18 in.
A large, chickenlike bird with a wide gray or rusty tail with a black band at the tip. Often flies up suddenly. Permanent resident.

GREAT CRESTED FLYCATCHER — 10 in.
A flycatcher with a grayish face, bright yellow belly, and rusty tail. Often perches high in the treetops. Voice a loud *wheep!*

RED-EYED VIREO — 6 in.
A greenish, slender bird with a white stripe above its red eyes and a gray crown. Searches upper branches for insects.

WOOD THRUSH — 9 in.
An upright thrush with a rusty head and heavily spotted breast. Song is flutelike, melodious. Winters in tropics.

OVENBIRD — 5 in.
A ground-dwelling wood warbler that walks rather than hops. Olive above, with a white eye ring and orange crown. Song a whistled, repeated *teacher!* Winters in tropics.

Widespread Birds of Western Forests

WILLIAMSON'S SAPSUCKER

WESTERN TANAGER

TOWNSEND'S SOLITAIRE

MOUNTAIN CHICKADEE

STELLER'S JAY

HAIRY WOODPECKER

BAND-TAILED PIGEON

PINE SISKIN

YELLOW-RUMPED WARBLER

DARK-EYED JUNCO

Oregon

Gray-headed

BLUE GROUSE

WHITE-CROWNED SPARROW

These 12 bird species can be found in many kinds of western forests.

WILLIAMSON'S SAPSUCKER   **9.5 in.**
A woodpecker. Male black with yellow belly, white wing patches, white rump. Female barred on back, lacks white wing patches.

WESTERN TANAGER   **7 in.**
Male yellow with black wings, tail, upper back. Red head. Female yellow with wing bars.

TOWNSEND'S SOLITAIRE   **8 in.**
A brown thrush with an eye ring, white outer tail feathers, and buffy orange on shoulders.

MOUNTAIN CHICKADEE   **5.75 in.**
An active bird, gray with black cap and throat, black line through eye.

HAIRY WOODPECKER   **9.5 in.**
Black and white, with unbarred white back. Males have a red spot on head. Also found in the East.

STELLER'S JAY   **13.5 in.**
Large crest, black head and upper parts, otherwise deep blue.

BAND-TAILED PIGEON   **15.5 in.**
Dark with lighter band at base of tail. White neck mark at close range.

PINE SISKIN   **5 in.**
Dark-streaked, pale yellow on wings. Also found in East.

BLUE GROUSE   **21 in.**
Male blue-gray with yellow "eyebrows." Females mottled brown.

YELLOW-RUMPED (AUDUBON'S) WARBLER   **6 in.**
Yellow rump and shoulder patch. Yellow throat in West. Eastern race, called Myrtle Warbler, has white throat.

DARK-EYED (OREGON) JUNCO   **6.75 in.**
Gray "hood," rich brown back, flanks. See eastern race on page 21.

DARK-EYED (GRAY-HEADED) JUNCO   **6.75 in.**
Pale gray with reddish back.

WHITE-CROWNED SPARROW   **7.5 in.**
Large, upright sparrow with bold white and black crown, pink bill.

Widespread
North American Mammals

ELK

WHITETAIL DEER

MULE
DEER

PRONGHORN

COYOTE

BISON

COLLARED
PECCARY

MOUNTAIN LION

BIGHORN SHEEP

GRIZZLY BEAR

BLACK BEAR

Some of these wide-ranging North American mammals are most common on the prairie.

ELK
Large deer with a buffy rump. Males have wide, many-pronged antler rack and shaggy mane on throat and neck. Females lack antlers. Western forests, mountain meadows.

WHITETAIL DEER
Common throughout most of North America. White "flag" under tail is conspicous when the animal is bounding away. Only males have antlers. Forests, mountain meadows.

MULE DEER
Similar to Whitetail Deer but with somewhat larger ears and a black tip on the tail. Common throughout much of the West.

PRONGHORN
White rump and white blazes on neck and face. Both sexes have horns. Western prairies. Often mistakenly called antelope.

BISON
Males have prominent humped shoulders, huge head, shaggy mane. Females smaller, less humped. Horns occur on both sexes.

BIGHORN SHEEP
Pale rump patch. Males with large, curved horns. Females with smaller, straighter horns. Western mountain meadows, peaks.

COLLARED PECCARY
Piglike; grayish black with pale shoulder stripe. Low-elevation forests, deserts, grasslands. Southwest.

MOUNTAIN LION
A large cat, uniformly tawny to grayish, with a long tail. Forests, particularly in mountainous areas. Rare, infrequently seen.

COYOTE
Doglike; grayish with rusty legs, feet, ears. Tail with black tip held down between legs when running. Common at lower elevations in the West, rapidly spreading eastward.

BLACK BEAR
Color ranges from black to brown to cinnamon. Large, with no tail. Often visits campsites, garbage dumps.

GRIZZLY BEAR
Brown, "grizzled" fur, humped shoulders, dish-shaped face. Uncommon except in Alaska, northwestern Canada.

Northern Hardwood Forest

Range: Eastern Canada and northern New England and New York, into the upper Midwest.

YELLOW BIRCH

YELLOW-BELLIED SAPSUCKER
male

DARK-EYED (SLATE-COLORED) JUNCO

EASTERN HEMLOCK

BLACK-THROATED BLUE WARBLER
male

WHITE PINE

SOLITARY VIREO

PAINTED TRILLIUM

STRIPED MAPLE

WHITE-THROATED SPARROW

The Northern Hardwood Forest is made up mostly of **Yellow Birch**, Sugar Maple (page 22), American Beech (page 22), **Eastern Hemlock,** and **White Pine.** The forest is known for its spectacular fall colors, when leaves turn yellow and deep orange. The forest is called "hardwood" for the Sugar Maples, birches, and American Beech, but the forest also has many softwood trees such as pines and hemlocks.

Yellow Birch has shiny, yellowish, papery bark. It grows fast, often in disturbed areas, and lives for a long time in the closed forest. Eastern White Pine also is a fast grower that quickly sprouts in disturbed areas. It has blue-green needles that grow in clusters of five, and long cones. Eastern Hemlock has short needles. It thrives in shaded, moist ravines. Shrubby **Striped Maple** is named for the pale green stripes in its bark. It is one of many small trees that grow in the understory. Many wildflower species carpet the forest floor, including the colorful **Painted Trillium,** identified by its three white petals with pink centers.

Numerous birds, most of which migrate south in the fall, nest among the hardwoods and hemlocks. The **Yellow-bellied Sapsucker** is a woodpecker that pecks rows of small holes in trees to get the sugary sap. The **Dark-eyed Junco** feeds on insects in summer but changes its diet to seeds in autumn, when juncos migrate south. The **White-throated Sparrow,** which also winters in southeastern states, whistles a melodious song: *Old Sam Peabody, Peabody, Peabody.* This husky sparrow is recognized by its bold white throat and head markings. The **Solitary Vireo** winters in Central America. It skulks through leaves in search of insects. Its most distinctive field marks are its bluish head and white eye ring. The **Black-throated Blue Warbler,** slate blue with a black throat, is found in the understory, snatching insects from leaves. Only the male is colorful; the female is drab brown and gray. Like the vireo, this warbler winters in Central America.

The most common mammals of the Northern Hardwood Forest are Whitetail Deer, Raccoon, Eastern Chipmunk, Striped Skunk, and Beaver.

Mid-Atlantic/Great Lakes Forest

Range: Southwestern New York through the upper Mid-Atlantic States to southern Minnesota, Wisconsin, Iowa.

CERULEAN WARBLER
male

SUGAR MAPLE

AMERICAN BEECH

BLACK-CAPPED CHICKADEE

ALTERNATE-LEAF DOGWOOD

AMERICAN BASSWOOD

fruit

American Beech, Sugar Maple, and **American Basswood** are the three broad-leaved tree species that define this deciduous forest community. These trees, in various combinations, dominate the forests of the Mid-Atlantic and southern Great Lakes areas. In many places, beech is the most numerous canopy tree, while Sugar Maple dominates the understory. Since Sugar Maple can grow in shade, it may eventually replace the beeches. This forest is best developed on moist sites, where there is sufficient water to support the big trees. In drier places, oaks and hickories tend to predominate.

American Beech has smooth, gray bark and oval leaves with large teeth along the margins. Beech leaves turn brown in fall, and many stay on the tree in winter. Though American Beech reproduces by making seeds (beech nuts), it also can sprout from roots. It is common to see a large beech surrounded by many smaller trees. Sugar Maple is one of the most magnificent and important trees in the East. It has broad, three-lobed leaves that turn brilliant orange in autumn. In spring, Sugar Maple sap is tapped and is used to make maple syrup. American Basswood, also called Linden, has oval leaves that are unsymmetrical at the base. Fruits hang in clusters from long, thin bracts. **Alternate-leaf Dogwood** usually grows as a shrub and is common in the understory. Its oval leaves alternate along the stem, rather than occurring in opposites as other dogwood leaves do. Many other shrubs, such as Mapleleaf Viburnum, Spicebush, and honeysuckles, are common in this forest.

The **Black-capped Chickadee** is among the most abundant resident birds. Its *chicka-dee-dee-dee* call can be heard in any month of the year. It is a little gray bird with a black head and black bib. In winter, they are among the commonest visitors to bird feeders. The **Cerulean Warbler** is a treetop species, one of several wood warblers that nest in broad-leaved trees. It can be difficult to see this bird well, as it tends to stay high in trees, but with patience and binoculars, it's possible. The male is light blue above and white below, and has a black band on its throat. The female is duller.

Appalachian Cove Forest

Range: Great Smoky Mountains, particularly in eastern Kentucky and Tennessee.

YELLOW BUCKEYE

YELLOWWOOD

TULIPTREE

WHITE BASSWOOD

FLAME AZALEA

CAROLINA SILVERBELL

HOODED WARBLER male

AMERICAN GINSENG

EASTERN REDBUD

WORM-EATING WARBLER

A cove is a small valley on the side of a mountain. More tree species occur in the lush, moist cove forests of central Appalachia than in any other place in all of North America. Most are broad-leaved, deciduous species such as **Tuliptree** and **White Basswood,** though conifers such as Eastern Hemlock may be found in sheltered ravines. Understory trees include **Eastern Redbud** and Flowering Dogwood, both of which add great bursts of color in early spring. There is usually a dense shrub layer of azaleas and rhododendrons, and more than 1,500 species of wildflowers grow here. The forest is cool and dark; the moist soil is ideal for the several dozen salamander species found along streambanks and under decaying logs.

Tuliptree, named for its large, tuliplike flower, can grow taller than 100 feet. White Basswood thrives in rich bottomland soil and is generally found only in cove forests. **Yellow Buckeye,** also called Sweet Buckeye, is similar to the much more widespread Ohio Buckeye but occurs only in a limited range in the moist cove forests. **Yellowwood** is one of 25 or 30 tree species that may join the basswoods and buckeyes of the cove forests. It is a small tree with sprays of white flowers. **Carolina Silverbell** is one of the most reliable indicator species of the cove forest. It too is a small tree, named for the delicate bell-shaped flowers that hang below its branches in spring. Eastern Redbud is an understory species that is unmistakable when in full bloom in spring, before the leaves have opened.

Flame Azalea is a brilliant orange-flowering shrub that is also found on mountain-top heath balds, places unique to Appalachia where trees are absent and shrubs prevail. **American Ginseng** has a thick, tuberous root containing a powerful chemical that is an effective defense in warding off attacks by insects and worms.

The sweet, whistled song of the **Hooded Warbler** and the buzzy trill of the **Worm-eating Warbler** are among the many bird sounds of cove forests during breeding season. Both warblers frequent the dense understory and can be seen with patient stalking.

Oak-Hickory Forest

Range: Southern New England and throughout the Southeast and Midwest.

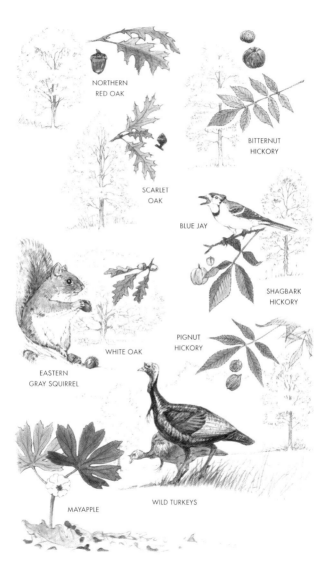

NORTHERN
RED OAK

BITTERNUT
HICKORY

SCARLET
OAK

BLUE JAY

SHAGBARK
HICKORY

PIGNUT
HICKORY

WHITE OAK

EASTERN
GRAY SQUIRREL

MAYAPPLE

WILD TURKEYS

This forest of broad-leaved, nut-producing trees is widespread on drier soils or south-facing slopes. Acorns and hickory nuts are usually obvious in the leaf litter on the forest floor. Roving flocks of **Blue Jays** moving noisily through the forest and ubiquitous **Eastern Gray Squirrels** are easy to find throughout the year. Fox Squirrels are also common, as are Eastern Chipmunks. In summer, tanagers sing from the treetops, while Ovenbirds and Wood Thrushes hunt for insects in the understory, made up mostly of Flowering Dogwood, Sassafras, and Hophornbeam. The forest lets in enough light to support a shrub layer of blueberries, huckleberries, viburnums, and laurels.

White Oak has one of the widest ranges of any tree species in eastern North America. Its leaves have rounded lobes without sharp tips. **Scarlet Oak** is named for the brilliant fall color of its leaves. **Northern Red Oak** leaves are duller red. Both species have leaves with sharp points on their lobes. Blue Jays feed heavily on acorns, and in years when acorns are abundant, jays bury them. Many oaks have been planted by Blue Jays.

Hickories are recognized by their compound leaves, with varying numbers of leaflets. **Pignut** and **Shagbark hickories** have similar leaves, but Shagbark has bark that peels in long strips. **Bitternut Hickory** has more leaflets than either Shagbark or Pignut. Hickory seeds are contained in thick hickory nuts, which are eaten by many animals, including Gray Squirrels and Wild Turkeys. Squirrel populations tend to vary with the abundance of nuts. In years when acorns or hickory nuts are abundant, expect to see many squirrels.

Mayapple is one of hundreds of wildflower species found in this widespread forest community. It has wide, umbrella-like leaves, with a big white flower hanging below like a bell. The fruit resembles a small apple.

Wild Turkeys were once extensively hunted but now are becoming more common in many areas. Because they are still hunted, they are often quite wary. Even though they are large birds, they can be hard to see in the dense understory.

Southern Hardwood Forest

Range: From the Carolinas south to the Gulf Coast, on rich soils.

TRUMPET CREEPER

TUFTED TITMOUSE

VIRGINIA LIVE OAK

NORTHERN MOCKINGBIRD

SPANISH MOSS

SOUTHERN MAGNOLIA

LAUREL OAK

SWEETBAY

RED-BELLIED WOODPECKER male

COMMON PERSIMMON

VIRGINIA OPOSSUM

PECAN

The Southern Hardwood Forest has a predominance of broad-leaved evergreen trees, many of which produce brilliant large flowers. Trees typically are draped with **Spanish Moss,** helping make this forest one of the most beautiful in North America. Spanish Moss is not a true moss but is part of a large family of mostly tropical plants that includes pineapples. It is an "air plant," or epiphyte, that grows on a branch of a tree but does no harm to its host.

Broad-leaved evergreens such as **Virginia Live Oak, Southern Magnolia,** and **Sweetbay** are common in the warm climate of the Deep South. Many of these trees are, like Spanish Moss, closely related to species found only in the tropics. **Common Persimmon,** Sweetbay, and Southern Magnolia have thick, waxy leaves that help reduce water loss from heat evaporation, a characteristic shared by most tropical plants. There are about 70 species of magnolias; all have large, attractive flowers. Close relatives of magnolias existed when the dinosaurs still lived, over 60 million years ago. Common Persimmon has flowers somewhat like magnolia, that become soft, juicy, sweet fruits. **Pecan,** a southern member of the hickory family, produces nutritious and tasty nuts. Oaks abound among the southern hardwoods, especially Virginia Live Oak and **Laurel Oak.** The former is especially characteristic of the coast and is known for its beautifully spreading shape. **Trumpet Creeper** is an often abundant vine that has long, red, tubular flowers attractive to hummingbirds and hawk moths.

The **Northern Mockingbird** and **Red-bellied Woodpecker** are two of the most common birds of the South. Mockingbirds, excellent mimics, often sing through the night. Both birds show conspicuous white wing patches as they fly.

The **Virginia Opossum** is the only marsupial found in North America. It gives birth to babies so tiny that a dozen will fit on a tablespoon. The babies move into a pouch on the mother's abdomen, where they suckle milk and continue to grow. The opossum has a prehensile tail (able to grasp) that allows the animal to hang upside down from a branch. When threatened, it "plays possum," appearing quite dead.

Northern Pine-Oak Forest

Range: New England through Virginia along the coastal plain, and west to the Great Lakes.

PINE WARBLER
male

BLACKJACK OAK

PITCH PINE

PRAIRIE WARBLER
male

VIRGINIA PINE

male

RUFOUS-SIDED TOWHEE

BEAR OAK

DWARF HUCKLEBERRY

BEARBERRY

The Northern Pine-Oak Forest is a scrubby coastal forest of trees that thrive on dry, sandy soils. The understory usually includes huckleberries and blueberries. Lightning-set fires are common. **Pitch Pine,** a northern tree, and **Virginia Pine,** which is more southern, are both small, often shrubby trees. Pitch Pine needles are in clusters of 3, and Virginia Pine needles are in clusters of 2. Both pines are relatively fire-resistant and sprout quickly from seeds in areas that have had recent fires. **Blackjack Oak** and **Bear Oak** are also similar trees. Both grow as small trees or shrubs, and both have thick, waxy leaves. Blackjack Oak leaves are wide, with golden undersides. Bear Oak leaves have somewhat deeper lobes and are silvery below. Other oaks eventually invade this pine-dominated forest, but fire does much more damage to the oaks than to the pines, so the pines continue to prevail in this type of forest.

Heaths are a large family of plants that grow best in acid soils such as those found in pine forests. **Dwarf Huckleberry** and **Bearberry** are two of many heaths that might be encountered. Dwarf Huckleberry has small, shiny leaves with tiny yellow resin dots. You will need to look closely to see the dots. The flowers are delicate and bell-like in shape. They dangle below the branches in little clusters. Bearberry is common in many areas in North America, including western mountains, where it is known as Kinnikinnick (see page 70). Bearberry grows as a spreading shrub, often covering much of the ground. Its flowers are pale pink or white.

The **Rufous-sided Towhee** is common throughout oak-pine woodlands and other forests. Towhees are actually large sparrows. They feed on the ground, kicking up litter with both legs simultaneously. The song of the towhee is described as *drink your tea...ah.* Two wood warblers, the **Pine Warbler** and **Prairie Warbler,** frequent the oak-pine forest. Pine Warblers live in the treetops, while Prairie Warblers prefer shrubby areas and power-line cuts. Both are yellow, but the Prairie has black streaking on its face and sides. The Pine Warbler sings a steady, repeated trill, while the Prairie's song is an insectlike buzz.

Southern Pine-Oak Forest

Range: Southeastern coastal plain from Virginia to Louisiana and eastern Texas.

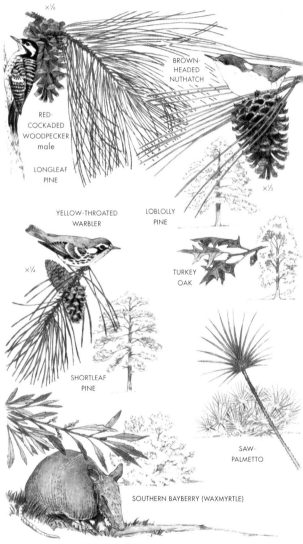

×⅙

RED-COCKADED WOODPECKER male

LONGLEAF PINE

BROWN-HEADED NUTHATCH

×⅓

LOBLOLLY PINE

YELLOW-THROATED WARBLER

×¼

TURKEY OAK

SHORTLEAF PINE

SAW-PALMETTO

SOUTHERN BAYBERRY (WAXMYRTLE)

NINE-BANDED ARMADILLO

Like its northern equivalent (see page 30), the Southern Pine-Oak Forest is typical of dry, sandy soils, which cover much of southeastern coastal regions. It is also a forest where occasional natural fires are essential to protect the pines from being replaced by oaks and other broad-leaved trees. **Longleaf Pine** adapts to fire extraordinarily well. Its seedlings, which resemble thick tufts of tall grass, put most of their energy into a deep tap root that fire can't reach. The long, grass-like needles help protect the seedling from fire damage. As adult trees, Longleaf Pines also have very long (18-inch) needles in clusters of 3. **Shortleaf Pine** needles are only a third as long and are mostly in clusters of 2. **Loblolly Pine** needles, in clusters of 3, are about 9 inches long. All three pines are common throughout most of the region and are often harvested for lumber.

Oaks of many species can be found with the pines, including **Turkey Oak,** a shrubby oak that rarely grows taller than 30 feet. Its leaves have deep, sharply pointed lobes. Other common oaks include Post, Laurel, Myrtle, and Southern Red oaks.

Unlike the northern pine-oak forest, the understory in this forest is poorly developed, consisting mainly of grass. The few shrubs that do occur include **Southern Bayberry,** also called Waxmyrtle. It can be identified by the pungent aroma of its crushed leaves. **Saw-palmetto** is a subtropical plant related to palms. Its large, fanlike leaves have very sharp edges; walking through a dense understory of Saw-Palmetto can prove a challenge.

Listen for the sweet, melodious whistle of the **Yellow-throated Warbler** in the treetops as it searches the pine needles for insects. This bird has a bright yellow throat and black face patch. Little bands of **Brown-headed Nuthatches** probe loose bark and pine cones in search of insects. The rare and endangered **Red-cockaded Woodpecker**, identified by its black and white ladder back and white cheek patch, lives only in old-growth pine forests.

The **Nine-banded Armadillo,** seen mostly at night, spends much of its time searching for ants and other insects (see page 52).

Northern Riverine Forest

Range: Throughout the northern and central regions of the Eastern Deciduous Forest.

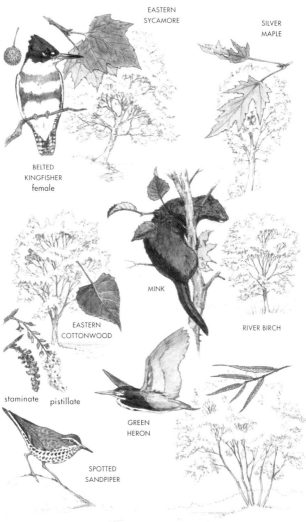

EASTERN SYCAMORE

SILVER MAPLE

BELTED KINGFISHER female

MINK

EASTERN COTTONWOOD

RIVER BIRCH

staminate   pistillate

GREEN HERON

SPOTTED SANDPIPER

BLACK WILLOW

Many kinds of trees are adapted to live along rivers, where annual spring flooding is common. These trees can tolerate having their roots underwater, at least for a few weeks a year. Most of them grow quickly when their seeds land on a newly exposed sand flat or mud bank. They thrive on flood plains, areas next to rivers where the rich sediments dropped by flood waters accumulate. As the trees grow, they help stabilize the area.

The **Eastern Sycamore** is an abundant flood plain species. Its bark peels in large brown flakes, revealing smooth white underneath. Its leaves are lobed like a maple's, and its seeds are contained in small ball-like fruits. The **Silver Maple** has deeply lobed leaves and pale, furrowed bark. Both **River Birch** and **Eastern Cottonwood** have unlobed leaves with teeth along the margins. Cottonwood leaves are more heart-shaped, on long stalks that make the leaves shiver in the slightest breeze. Cottonwood seeds are attached to cottony fibers that help carry the seeds in the wind. **Black Willow** leaves are thin and lance-like. Willows, which grow in dense, shrubby clusters, are often the first to colonize a newly created sandbar.

Rivers attract many species of birds and mammals. The **Belted Kingfisher** is one of the few bird species in which females are more colorful than males. Only the female has the orangy breast band. Kingfishers dive head first for fish and build their nests at the end of tunnels dug in embankments. The crow-sized **Green Heron** stalks fish and other water animals in shallow areas, snatching its prey with a quick strike of its flexible neck and strong beak. The robin-sized **Spotted Sandpiper** bobs its tail, constantly teetering as it walks deliberately along, picking insects and other small animals from among the rocks. Spotted Sandpipers have spotted breasts only during the breeding season.

The **Mink** is a common but seldom seen predator, a member of the weasel family. Minks are slender, with a long, hairy tail. They are like smaller versions of River Otters (page 54), but, unlike otters, minks are not very social. They are usually seen one at a time.

Southern Riverine Forest

Range: From Maryland, Virginia, and the Carolinas southward, along streams and rivers.

BOX-ELDER (ASHLEAF MAPLE)

NORTHERN CARDINAL   male

SOUTHERN ARROWWOOD

BARRED OWL

SWAMP WHITE OAK

SMOOTH (TAG) ALDER

WOOD DUCK male

RIVER BIRCH

SWEETGUM

BUTTONBUSH

LOUISIANA WATERTHRUSH

Riverine forests perform important ecological functions. Because the growing season is long and the soil is rich, these forests produce a great deal of nutritious plant material, which helps support the many animals that live here. Much of this material is eventually recycled, some of it going downriver into other habitats. Riverine forests also absorb flood waters.

Box-elder, also called Ashleaf Maple, is the only maple with compound leaves, each of which has three leaflets. **Swamp White Oak** has a wide, spreading crown with drooping branches. Its leaves are pale whitish below. **Sweetgum** is abundant in moist soils throughout much of the Southeast. Its star-shaped leaves and distinct seed balls make it easy to identify. **Smooth Alder, Buttonbush,** and **Southern Arrowwood** are common shrubs in riverine forests, often growing in dense thickets along the river. Alder has drooping catkins, and Buttonbush has flowers in ball-like clusters. Arrowwood, a member of the widespread Viburnum family, produces clusters of deep blue-black fruits that birds love.

The **Barred Owl** is an abundant resident of swamps and riverine forests. Its characteristic loud, hooting call, *Who cooks for you,* is one of the most distinctive nighttime sounds of the South. Pairs of Barred Owls often hoot back and forth to one another. The brilliant red **Northern Cardinal** male is unmistakable. It is often seen perched atop a tree or shrub singing a loud, whistled *Cheer, cheer!* or *Purty, purty, purty.* The colorful **Wood Duck** is sometimes shy, flying up from the river with a shrieking *Wheek!* Wood Ducks nest in tree cavities. Although they are large birds, they are skilled at flying through dense forest without hitting branches. The loud, warbled whistle of the **Louisiana Waterthrush** is another characteristic bird song of the Southern Riverine Forest. This bird may be seen searching for food among the rocks and pebbles that line streams. As it searches, it constantly bobs its tail, a characteristic it shares with the Spotted Sandpiper (pages 34, 106). The similar Northern Waterthrush has more streaks on its throat and a more yellowish breast.

Northern Swamp Forest

Range: Northeastern states through the Midwest.

WILLOW
OAK

ATLANTIC
WHITE-CEDAR

CEDAR
WAXWING

BLACK
TUPELO
(BLACK GUM)

RED MAPLE

SWEET
PEPPERBUSH

× 2

SPICEBUSH

SKUNK
CABBAGE

A swamp is a forest that is water-logged for a good portion of the year. Trees and other plants that live here must be able to withstand having their roots underwater, where there is lots of mud and little oxygen. **Atlantic White-Cedar** is a needle-leaved tree that grows so abundantly in places that these areas are known as "cedar swamps." In the Midwest, it is replaced by the similar Northern White-Cedar. White-Cedars have blue-green, scale-like leaves that feel prickly. The cones are small bluish balls.

Willow Oak is named for its thin, pencil-like leaves, which resemble willow leaves. However, no willow makes acorns, as this oak does.

Black Tupelo, also called Black Gum, is identified by its smooth, glossy, oval leaves. In late summer and early fall, the tree fills with clusters of blue-black fruits that attract songbirds. Tupelo fruits are highly nutritious, filled with fat that provides energy for migrating birds. Large flocks of **Cedar Waxwings** often gather in tupelos and other fruiting trees. These gregarious birds are the most fruit-loving of any North American bird species. They are permanent residents throughout much of the country, but they move around locally in search of fruits.

The **Red Maple** is named for the bright red color of its autumn leaves. Red Maples often dominate swamp forests in the Northeast. Though they tolerate wetness, they also do well on dry sites, including mountain ridges. Like all maples, its seeds are contained in long "wings," which are reddish in this species.

Sweet Pepperbush and **Spicebush** are shrubs that can be abundant in the understory of swamp forests. Sweet Pepperbush has white flower clusters at the branch tips. A careful look will reveal that flowers open from the bottom of the stalk upward. Spicebush has smooth, shiny leaves that emit a pungent, pleasant aroma when broken. Small yellowish flowers along the branches become red berries in fall. Like tupelo, Spicebush fruits are sought after by migrating songbirds.

Skunk Cabbage is easily recognized by its large, cabbage-like leaves that give off an unpleasant odor when crushed. It is one of the first plants to come up in spring.

Southern Hardwood Swamp Forest

Range: Throughout the Southeast from Virginia to eastern Texas.

SWAMP OAK

SUMMER TANAGER

male

OVERCUP OAK

WATER OAK

SOUTHERN RED OAK

AMERICAN HOLLY

CAROLINA WREN

fruit

PAWPAW

Deciduous oaks are dominant in this southern forest of wet, water-logged soils. Baldcypress, Black Tupelo, and Sweetgum (page 36) may also occur, and there are usually many vines, such as White Clematis (page 72) and Trumpet Creeper (page 28). **Swamp Oak** is a widespread oak, identified by its leaves with many shallow lobes. **Overcup Oak,** like Swamp Oak, has a tall, spreading crown and may reach a height of 80 feet. Its leaves have smooth, deep, irregular lobes. **Water Oak,** named for its tolerance of wet soils, can reach 100 feet tall and has distinctive oblong leaves, unlobed and wavy on the edges. **Southern Red Oak** has sharply pointed lobes that are widest in the middle of the leaf. The leaves turn deep red in fall. This species can be found in uplands as well as swamps.

The understory of a southern hardwoods swamp often has a dense shrub layer of **American Holly** and **Pawpaw.** American Holly is one of the most easily recognized plants, with evergreen leaves that have sharp tips, and bright red berries often used in Yuletide decorations. Pawpaw grows as a small tree or as a dense thicket of shrubs. Its large, tasty fruits are eaten by many species of birds and mammals, including Wild Turkeys (page 26). Pawpaw is the only member of its tropical plant family to occur so far north.

Singing its melodious warbled song from atop an oak, the all-red male **Summer Tanager** is easy to identify. The female (not shown) is bright yellow. Pairs often forage together for caterpillers and other insect food. From the understory, you can hear the loud, ringing *Cheedala, cheedala, cheedala!* that announces the presence of a **Carolina Wren.** This common wren of the South is warm brown with a pale stripe over its eye.

Among the many other birds of southern swamp forests are Barred Owls, Wood Ducks, Pileated Woodpeckers, Yellow-billed Cuckoos, and Prothonotary, Parula, and Yellow warblers. Water-loving reptiles include many turtles, snakes, and American Alligator (page 42).

Baldcypress Swamp Forest

Range: Coasts from Maryland to Texas, including Florida and the Gulf Coast.

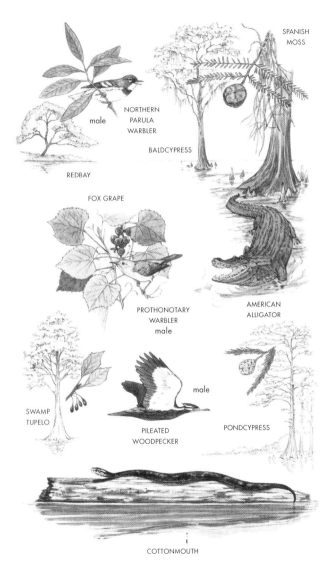

SPANISH MOSS

NORTHERN PARULA WARBLER
male

BALDCYPRESS

REDBAY

FOX GRAPE

PROTHONOTARY WARBLER
male

AMERICAN ALLIGATOR

SWAMP TUPELO

PILEATED WOODPECKER
male

PONDCYPRESS

COTTONMOUTH

Tall **Baldcypresses** draped with Spanish Moss give this swampy forest an eerie, primeval look. This is a true swamp forest, usually too wet to hike through easily. Large tracts of Baldcypress Swamp are refuges for Cougars, Bobcats, Black Bears, and many species of wading birds such as herons and egrets.

Baldcypress trees grow fast, even in the water-logged soils of the swamp, and can reach heights of 100 feet. Cypresses are needle-leaved trees that shed their needles in fall and grow new ones the following spring. The cones are rounded and berrylike. Cypress "knees" are roots that protrude above the water and may help the tree get oxygen. The similar **Pondcypress** is common in stagnant swamps. **Swamp Tupelo** is a variety of tupelo common in southern coastal swamps. **Redbay** is a small evergreen tree with a wide, often irregular crown. Wherever sunlight is abundant, especially along rivers, vines abound, including **Fox Grape,** with broad, heart-shaped leaves and tempting violet grapes.

The loud *whicka-whacka-whacka* of the crow-sized **Pileated Woodpecker** is often heard in the swamp. The Pileated, which shows broad white underwings in flight, is similar to the larger and extinct Ivory-billed Woodpecker that once lived in cypress swamps. Two warblers are common among the cypresses. The **Northern Parula Warbler** sings its insectlike buzzing song from the treetops, where it builds its tiny nest from Spanish Moss. Males have an orangy red band across their upper breast. The brilliant orange **Prothonotary Warbler** sings its loud, whistled song from the understory, where it nests in tree cavities.

Many snakes live in the swamp, among them the poisonous **Cottonmouth,** named for its white mouth—seen only by those who come too close. It senses prey with heat-detecting cells in pits on its snout. Like its relatives, rattlesnakes and copperheads, it has a triangular head. The **American Alligator,** the largest reptile in the swamp, can reach a length of 15 feet. Males bellow loudly during mating season. Females build nests, laying 10 to 50 eggs, which they guard closely until they hatch.

Subtropical Forest

Range: Southern Florida, especially around Everglades National Park.

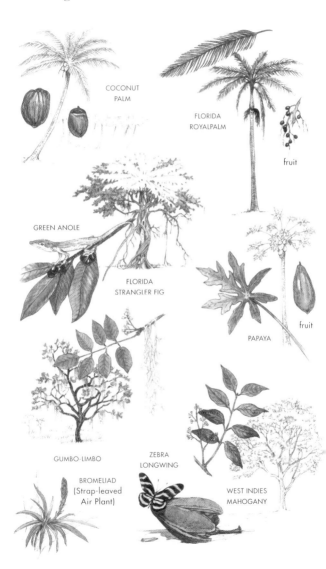

COCONUT PALM

FLORIDA ROYALPALM

fruit

GREEN ANOLE

FLORIDA STRANGLER FIG

PAPAYA

fruit

GUMBO-LIMBO

ZEBRA LONGWING

BROMELIAD (Strap-leaved Air Plant)

WEST INDIES MAHOGANY

The Subtropical Forest, found only in southern Florida, is a mix of West Indian, Caribbean, and North American species. It occurs on raised areas of land called hammocks, forest islands among the vast marshes of Everglades sawgrass. The growing season lasts virtually all year, and most of the trees are evergreen. The Subtropical Forest has many of the characteristics of tropical forests, including plenty of colorful butterflies, birds, and reptiles.

Palms are abundant. The tall **Florida Royalpalm** reaches 100 feet, its trunk ending in a wide green stem from which 10-foot-long fronds grow. The **Coconut Palm** grows in the tropics throughout the world, producing large nuts that contain sweet "milk" and delicious white fruit. **Papayas** are not palms but are sometimes mistaken for them because their wide-lobed leaves grow in clusters similar to palm fronds. Papaya fruits are orange and considered among the tastiest tropical fruits. Other broad-leaved trees include the **Gumbo Limbo,** easily identified by its bright red, smooth bark, and the **West Indies Mahogany,** with its dark compound leaves and rough brown bark.

The odd **Florida Strangler Fig,** found thoughout the world's tropics, begins life as a tiny vine whose seed was dropped on a branch by a bird. The Strangler grows and spreads throughout the tree, eventually surrounding the trunk of its host tree and often killing it. **Bromeliads** are tropical air plants in the pineapple family. They grow on the branches of host trees but do no harm. Leaves are sharp and stiff. Bromeliads are closely related to the widespread Spanish Moss (page 28).

The slender-winged **Zebra Longwing** is a brilliant yellow and black butterfly that is poisonous to birds. As a caterpillar, it feeds on passionflower vines, which contain poisons that make both the caterpillar and the adult butterfly unpalatable and toxic to birds. The bright colors of the adult butterfly warn birds to leave it alone.

The **Green Anole** is an abundant lizard throughout the Southeast. It is usually green but can change to brown when resting on bark.

Mangrove Swamp Forest

Range: Extreme south coastal Florida and throughout the West Indies and Caribbean.

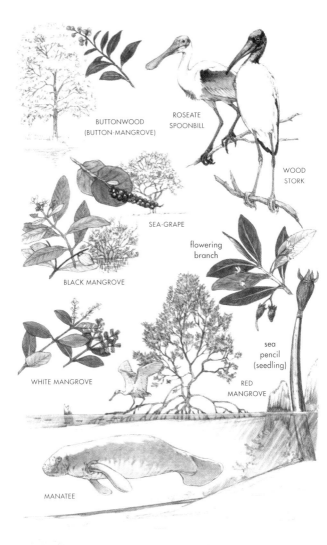

BUTTONWOOD
(BUTTON-MANGROVE)

ROSEATE
SPOONBILL

WOOD
STORK

SEA-GRAPE

flowering
branch

BLACK MANGROVE

sea
pencil
(seedling)

WHITE MANGROVE

RED
MANGROVE

MANATEE

Mangroves are tropical, saltwater-tolerant trees, mostly small in size. Mangroves have in common their ability to survive along hot, salty tropical coasts. **Red Mangrove,** named for its reddish bark and prop roots, is often the most abundant species. It hugs coastlines and colonizes sandbars, often stabilizing the sand and helping form a new island. Its flowers are quite small, but they develop into pencil-sized seedling pods that can float many miles in the ocean until they strike land. Its "prop roots" help anchor the plant in the shifting sand. **Black Mangrove** forms dense thickets on mudflats, usually beyond the line of Red Mangroves. Black Mangrove roots send up scores of fingerlike extensions that help the plant receive oxygen. **White Mangrove** is much less tolerant of saltwater than the other two species and is usually found in smaller numbers, growing on raised areas well away from the sea. **Buttonwood,** or Button-Mangrove, has tiny green flowers and small, buttonlike fruits. It also grows away from direct exposure to seawater. All mangroves have thick, leathery leaves, an adaptation for resisting water loss from evaporation. **Sea-Grape** has the thickest, most rounded leaves of any coastal tree. Its purple fruits grow in grapelike clusters.

Many colorful wading birds inhabit mangrove swamps, often in dense colonies on islands. The **Roseate Spoonbill** is unmistakable, a bright pink bird with a long bill widened at the tip like a huge spoon. Spoonbills skim their bills through the water and mud, capturing small fish and other water animals. The tall **Wood Stork** is the only true stork in North America. This threatened species survives only in small colonies from Florida to Texas. Wood Storks often soar in flocks during the day, their necks extended, and are all white with black wing linings. Their naked heads are gray, and their bills are long and somewhat curved.

The odd **Manatee** is a large, gray mammal of the mangroves and weed-infested waterways. Manatees have a doglike head, paddlelike forefeet, and a large, flat tail. Manatees are slow, gentle animals that feed on underwater vegetation, especially Water Hyacinth.

Texas Lower Rio Grande Forest 1
(see also page 50)

Range: Extreme south Texas from Harlingen to Brownsville.

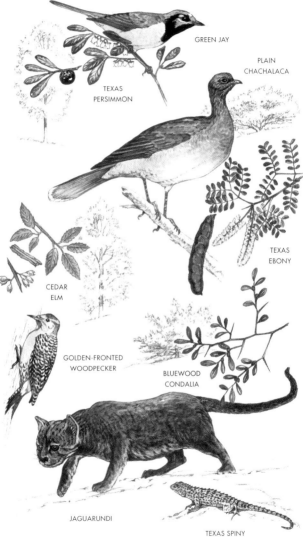

GREEN JAY

PLAIN
CHACHALACA

TEXAS
PERSIMMON

TEXAS
EBONY

CEDAR
ELM

GOLDEN-FRONTED
WOODPECKER

BLUEWOOD
CONDALIA

JAGUARUNDI

TEXAS SPINY
LIZARD

This is a hot, dry, subtropical forest, with summer temperatures often over 100°F. Because of the dry climate (only 25 inches of rain per year), the forest consists of small trees and shrubs, many of which are spiny. In many places trees are laden with Spanish Moss (page 28) and other air plants. Many trees and shrubs are legumes, members of the huge pea and bean family, with delicate compound leaves and seeds in pods. Today, only about 5% of the natural habitat of the Lower Rio Grande Valley remains, but these small tracts are habitat for a diverse array of species more characteristic of Mexico than of the United States.

Where the forest borders the Rio Grande are remnant lakes called *resacas*, which were once part of the flowing waters of the Rio Grande. **Cedar Elm,** identified by its arrow-shaped, toothed leaves, grows abundantly. **Jerusalem-thorn,** also called Retama, is common as well, recognized by its smooth green bark and long sharp thorns on whiplike branches. The yellow flowers resemble those of peas.

The large, 16-inch **Ringed Kingfisher** courses over the quiet waters of the resacas, uttering its harsh, rattling call. This species is common in Central and South America.

Farther from the river is upland forest, called *monte* or *matorral.* This forest is drier, and trees are shorter than along the river, mostly thorn-bearing trees such as **Texas Ebony.** Named for its dark wood, it has a spreading crown, evergreen, oval leaflets, and bright yellow flower clusters that attract many insects. **Great Lead-tree,** also called Tepeguaje, has feathery, fern-like leaflets and smooth bark. Its white flower clusters become long, thin, flattened seed pods, with pealike seeds bulging inside. **Texas Persimmon** is a close relative of the more widely distributed Common Persimmon (page 28). **Spiny Hackberry,** also called Granjeno, is identified by its dark, evergreen, toothed leaves and sharp thorns. **Bluewood Condalia,** also called Brazil, forms dense, spiny thickets that afford excellent protection for wildlife.

Many of the birds of the Lower Rio Grande forest are mainly found in Mexico. The **Plain Chachalaca** is named for its loud, unmusical

RINGED
KINGFISHER

ALTAMIRA
ORIOLE

JERUSALEM-THORN

KISKADEE

GREAT
LEADTREE

OCELOT

SPINY
HACKBERRY

SPECKLED RACER

TEXAS
TORTOISE

cha-cha-lac call, often given simultaneously by a flock of a dozen or more birds. Most chachalacas occur in Central and South America. The **Kiskadee** is also named for its loud, ringing voice *(kisk-a-dee!)*. It is widespread and abundant throughout tropical America. Look for the Great Kiskadee near water. In addition to flying from a perch to capture flying insects, Great Kiskadees will often snatch fish as a kingfisher does. The **Green Jay** is identified by its green color and yellow outer tail feathers, which are conspicuous in flight. Green Jays range south into Ecuador, but in the U.S. they live only in the Lower Rio Grande Valley. During breeding season they are somewhat secretive, but they are otherwise conspicuous and easily attracted to bird feeders. The large 10-inch **Altamira Oriole** is an almost electric orange alternating with black. Like other oriole species, it builds a long, basketlike nest suspended from a branch tip. The **Golden-fronted Woodpecker** ranges from Mexico into northern Texas. These birds are often seen on telephone poles and fence posts.

Two tropical cats, **Ocelot** and **Jaguarundi,** are both endangered species. Ocelots, which resemble small Jaguars, once ranged throughout Texas into southernmost Oklahoma and central Arizona. Their numbers have been drastically reduced by habitat loss and persecution, though today they are fully protected by law. The Jaguarundi is a slender, unspotted cat, usually dark-colored, with a long tail. Jaguarundis are sometimes active in daylight but are rare in Lower Rio Grande forests.

The **Texas Tortoise** is a reptile that is usually active at night, spending most of the hot daytime hours in a burrow. The **Texas Spiny Lizard** is a pale, long-legged lizard with rough spines. Sixteen species of spiny lizards occur within the United States, and most are found in the Southwest. This species ranges from eastern Mexico into northern Texas. All spiny lizards eat insects and other arthropods. The **Speckled Racer** is another Mexican species. Racers are active during the day, are very fast, and are not poisonous.

Texas Edwards Plateau Forest

Range: Limited to central Texas.

GOLDEN-CHEEKED
WARBLER

AGARITA

ASHE
JUNIPER

BLACK-CAPPED
VIREO

VIRGINIA
LIVE OAK

LACEY
OAK

LADDER-BACKED
WOODPECKER

EASTERN
PRICKLY-PEAR

NORTHERN
BOBWHITE

NINE-BANDED
ARMADILLO

FIREWHEEL

The Edwards Plateau, part of the Texas hill country, is a land of juniper-covered hillsides, limestone soils, scrubby oaks, abundant wildflowers, and canyons rich with riverine species such as Cedar Elm and Baldcypress. The plateau is located in central Texas, from Austin and San Antonio west to Fort Stockton and Midland. Because of low annual rainfall (10–30 inches), most forests consist of small trees and scattered shrubs, especially **Ashe Juniper, Virginia Live Oak,** and **Lacey Oak,** which often grow abundantly on hillsides. Dense stands of Ashe Juniper are called "cedar brakes." The small, wide-spreading oaks are often laden with Ball Moss, an air plant (epiphyte) related to the tropical bromeliads. From spring through summer, wildflower species such as the brilliant **Firewheel** grow in splendid displays. Over 400 species of wildflowers have been found on the plateau, including several that are found nowhere else.

Agarita is among the most common shrubs of the plateau. Its leaves are sharply lobed and hollylike. Blooms of yellow flowers occur from February to April, followed by bright red berrylike fruits. Agarita leaves are so sharply pointed that they remind the careless walker of cactus. True cacti, such as **Eastern Pricklypear,** are also common.

Two endangered bird species, the **Golden-cheeked Warbler** and the **Black-capped Vireo,** nest on the Edwards Plateau. Indeed, the Golden-cheeked Warbler nests nowhere else. It depends on Ashe Juniper for nesting material, lining its nest with strips of the bark. An interesting combination of eastern and western birds is also found on the plateau. For instance, a **Ladder-backed Woodpecker,** a southwestern species, may be drilling on a dead oak, at the base of which is a **Northern Bobwhite,** a bird typical of eastern pastures.

Mammals include the **Nine-banded Armadillo,** Whitetail Deer, and Fox Squirrel. The armadillo, common on the plateau, is related to the anteaters and sloths of South America. It is mostly hairless, its skin hard and bonelike. When threatened, the animal curls into a tight ball, protected by its bony armor.

Midwestern Prairie Riverine Forest

Range: Prairie-forest border in Illinois, Iowa, Missouri, and Arkansas, extending along major rivers through Oklahoma, Kansas, Nebraska, and the Dakotas.

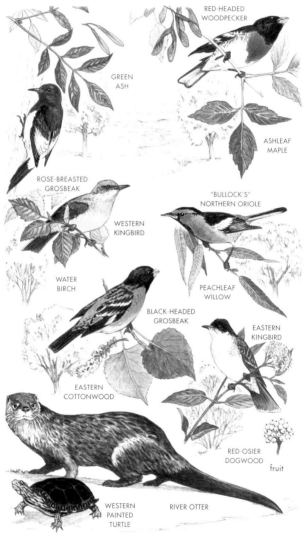

RED-HEADED WOODPECKER

GREEN ASH

ASHLEAF MAPLE

ROSE-BREASTED GROSBEAK

"BULLOCK'S" NORTHERN ORIOLE

WESTERN KINGBIRD

WATER BIRCH

PEACHLEAF WILLOW

BLACK-HEADED GROSBEAK

EASTERN KINGBIRD

EASTERN COTTONWOOD

RED-OSIER DOGWOOD

fruit

WESTERN PAINTED TURTLE

RIVER OTTER

The Prairie Riverine Forest borders the great western river systems—the Platte, Missouri, and Arkansas rivers—that flow east to eventually drain into the Mississippi. Moisture provided by the rivers enables tall trees to grow where, away from the river, there is dry prairie grassland. The common trees are willows, **Green Ash, Ashleaf Maple** (see Box-elder, page 36), **Water Birch, Eastern Cottonwood,** and **Plains Cottonwood,** all of which thrive under wet conditions. Stately groves of tall, widely spaced cottonwoods harbor a rich understory of wildflowers. In other areas, dense, almost jungly clumps of **Peachleaf Willow** grow, along with Green Ash and thickets of **Red-osier Dogwood,** Smooth Sumac, and Buttonbush. Vines such as bittersweet, honeysuckle, grape, and Virginia Creeper are often abundant. Where rivers are wide and winding, look for sandbars colonized by thickets of Sandbar Willow.

The prairie riverine forest hosts a mix of eastern and western species. An **Eastern Kingbird** may share a utility wire with a **Western Kingbird. Rose-breasted Grosbeaks** and **Black-headed Grosbeaks** may sing loudly in the same cottonwood grove. The pendulous nest of an oriole may be inhabited by a pair of the **"Bullock's"** race of **Northern Oriole,** or a pair of the "Baltimore" race—or a female "Baltimore" and male "Bullock's"! The boldly patterned **Red-headed Woodpecker** has been reduced in numbers over much of its range, probably by nest site competition with European Starlings. Red-heads are still common, however, in midwestern riverine forest.

River Otters range throughout most of North America. Otters are aquatic members of the weasel tribe, making their homes by excavating dens in embankments. Otters are renowned for their apparent pleasure at frolicking, especially sliding down muddy banks. They eat fish, crayfish, frogs, and whatever other animals they can capture.

The **Western Painted Turtle** is the most common turtle species in the Prairie Riverine habitat. It can often be seen sunning itself on exposed logs and rocks.

Black Hills Forest

Range: Southwestern South Dakota, extending into eastern Wyoming.

BLUE JAY

DARK-EYED JUNCO

WHITE SPRUCE

PONDEROSA PINE

LEWIS'S WOODPECKER

AMERICAN ELM

BUR OAK

BOHEMIAN WAXWING

ROCKY MOUNTAIN JUNIPER

BIRCHLEAF CERCOCARPUS

RED SQUIRREL

SHRUBBY CINQUEFOIL

ROCK WREN

In the high plains of the Midwest, mainly in southwestern South Dakota, the Black Hills are an area of low mountains surrounded by seas of prairie grassland. The name "Black Hills" refers to the dark look created by stands of **Ponderosa Pine** and **White Spruce** (page 59) against the light-colored prairie grasses. Ponderosa Pine predominates in most places, while White Spruce grows where conditions are cooler and wetter. Along streams and rivers, deciduous trees such as willows, cottonwoods, **Bur Oak,** Green Ash (page 54), and **American Elm** are found. At lower elevations, the Black Hills forest meets prairie grassland, with abundant grass and wildflower species. Shrubs such as Big Sagebrush (page 64) and Tall Rabbitbrush are common on the prairie, with **Shrubby Cinquefoil** and **Birchleaf Cercocarpus** (also called Mountain-mahogany) growing densely in rocky areas. Ponderosa Pine would eventually replace much of the grassland were it not for natural fires, usually set by summer lightning, that burn back the pines and preserve the grassland.

The Black Hills regularly host 139 species of birds, some typically western, some eastern in range. Burned-over Ponderosa Pine stands provide habitat for **Lewis's Woodpecker,** which ranges widely over the West. The white-winged form of the **Dark-eyed Junco** (page 21), once considered a separate species, occurs only in the Black Hills. **Rock Wrens** frequent rugged outcrops among hillsides of **Rocky Mountain Juniper,** and in winter, large flocks of wandering **Bohemian Waxwings** can be seen.

Red Squirrels are abundant among the pines, and large mammals such as Elk, Mule Deer, and Whitetail Deer are common. Small herds of Bison and Pronghorn inhabit the grasslands along with colonies of Blacktail Prairie Dogs.

The Black Hills are rich in both natural and human history. Gold was discovered here in the 1870s, leading quickly to the eviction of the Lakota Sioux Indians and eventually resulting in the Battle of Little Bighorn in southern Montana, where Sitting Bull soundly defeated General George Custer.

Boreal Forest
(see also page 60)

Range: Extreme northern New England, Wisconsin, Minnesota, Michigan, and most of Canada and Alaska.

WHITE-WINGED
CROSSBILL
male

GRAY
JAY

WHITE
SPRUCE

BLACKBURNIAN
WARBLER

male

BALSAM
FIR

TAMARACK
(AMERICAN LARCH)

RED
SQUIRREL

MOOSE

PAPER
BIRCH

CANADA MAYFLOWER

The Boreal Forest extends throughout the northernmost regions of the lower 48 states, plus most of Canada and Alaska. It is a vast forest of "Christmas trees" dominated by huge numbers of firs, spruces, **Tamarack,** and other conifers. Trees and animals of the Boreal Forest must contend with a climate with a very short growing season and long, cold, often snowy winters. The conical shapes of most of the conifers helps these trees shed their burdens of snow in the strong, cold winds.

The region of the Boreal Forest was entirely under the ice of glaciers as recently as 15,000 years ago. The glaciers have since receded, but their signatures remain in the forms of seemingly innumerable lakes and bogs scattered among the conifer forests. Fire is no stranger to the northern forest, and many plants have developed adaptations that help them survive periodic blazes.

White Spruce is recognized by its four-sided, stiff, blue-green needles that tend to curve upward along the branches. **Balsam Fir,** with its rich, pungent fragrance, is one of the species most commonly sold as Christmas trees. **Jack Pine** is a widespread tree of poor, sandy soils, especially burned areas. This tree is especially well adapted to periodic wildfires: it holds its cones on the tree, tightly closed, for many years, until the heat of fire releases the seeds inside. Moist areas frequently contain dense thickets of **Speckled Alder** and **Sitka Alder**. Deciduous trees of the Boreal Forest include **Paper Birch,** easily identified by its distinctive white, peeling bark. This species was used extensively by Native Americans for making canoes and is favored by Beavers for dams and lodges.

Many wildflowers can be found in and around the Boreal Forest. **Mountain Lady's-slipper** is a common large orchid with a white lip, purple side petals, and a yellow center. **Orange Hawkweed** is an abundant, colorful, open-area species found along roadsides and throughout disturbed areas. **Canada Mayflower** often carpets the shady forest floor, producing delicate white blossoms in spring.

In the trees, **Gray Jays** and **White-winged**

Boreal Forest
(see also page 58)

BLACKPOLL
WARBLER

JACK
PINE

WHITE
SPRUCE

SPRUCE
GROUSE

SPECKLED
ALDER

SITKA
ALDER

LYNX

WOLVERINE

ORANGE HAWKWEED

MOUNTAIN
LADY'S-SLIPPER

Crossbills are common, as well as other bird species, including the chickenlike **Spruce Grouse.** In summer, many colorful wood warblers arrive to feed and nest among the conifers, such as the **Blackpoll Warbler** and **Blackburnian Warbler,** both of which make the long migration from the American tropics.

Among the mammals here are **Red Squirrels,** Porcupines, Snowshoe Hares, and Black Bears. The unmistakable **Moose** is the largest of the world's deer: males measure fully 10 feet long and stand 6 feet tall at the shoulder, with a wide, thick rack of antlers. A large male can weigh in at about 1,400 pounds. The Moose has a very long face, which lets the animal feed on shallow underwater plants without completely submerging its head. The Boreal Forest is often called the "Spruce-Moose" forest.

Two impressive predatory mammals are essentially confined to the Boreal Forest. The husky **Lynx** is a boreal cat with conspicuously large paws, an adaptation for hunting on snow. Lynx run swiftly and feed mostly on Snowshoe Hares (page 74). The other predator is rarely seen and unlike any other in the Boreal Forest. It is an extremely large weasel, so large, in fact, that it resembles a small, shaggy bear. This animal, often called "the glutton," is more properly named the **Wolverine.** Identified by its large size (over 40 inches) and shaggy, yellow-banded fur, the Wolverine has earned a reputation as the most ferocious animal of the Boreal Forest. It can drive larger predators, even Black Bears and Mountain Lions, off their prey. Most people never get to see a wild Wolverine. It is a thrilling and elusive beast.

Boreal Bog

Range: Scattered throughout the Boreal Forest in the northern United States, Canada, and Alaska.

OLIVE-SIDED FLYCATCHER

BLACK SPRUCE

NASHVILLE WARBLER

male

LEATHER-LEAF

LABRADOR-TEA

RUSTY BLACKBIRD

× 1½

NORTHERN GREEN ORCHIS

ROUND-LEAVED SUNDEW

PITCHER-PLANT

Bogs are wetland habitats, usually within Boreal Forest. Bogs, also called muskeg, are former open ponds that are now slowly filling. They may or may not contain open water. Sphagnum Moss is abundant throughout most of the bog, and shrubs such as **Laborador-tea** and **Leatherleaf** are usually abundant along the edges. **Black Spruce** and Tamarack appear as the bogs fill. Bogs are intrinsically unstable; the term "quaking bog" refers to the odd feeling one has when walking on a bog, as the ground below ripples with your footsteps.

Specialties of bog habitats include colorful and delicate orchids, such as the tall **Northern Green Orchis,** as well as insect-eating plants, such as **Pitcher-plant** and **Round-leaved Sundew.** Both Pitcher-plant and Sundew trap flies and other insects, using the animals as a source of needed nitrogen.

Bogs are ideal habitats for such species as Moose, otters, minks, and Muskrats. Some bird species, including the **Nashville Warbler** and **Rusty Blackbird,** nest only at bog edges. Other birds, such as the **Olive-sided Flycatcher,** commonly feed in and around bogs.

Most bogs form in depressions left by retreating glaciers. Bog waters are usually dark brown, the color of strong tea, and very acidic. The color is caused by the slow accumulation of chemicals called tannins from leaves that drop into the bog.

Many Boreal Bogs have recognizable zones around their edges. The outermost, driest zone contains trees characteristic of normal Boreal Forest. Next comes a zone of bog-favoring trees, the Tamaracks and Black Spruce. The next zone is that of the bog shrubs, Leatherleaf and Laborador-tea. The shrub zone may be very dense and often includes alders as well. The inner zone consists of Sphagnum Moss, orchids, and insect-eating plants. There may be a small zone of open water in the center of the bog, depending upon how much the bog has filled. Over thousands of years, the outer zones move progressively inward, eclipsing and replacing the inner zones, until the bog is completely filled and no bog species remain. This is an example of a long-term ecological succession.

Rocky Mountain Pinyon/Juniper Forests

Range: Central and southern Rockies at low to middle elevations.

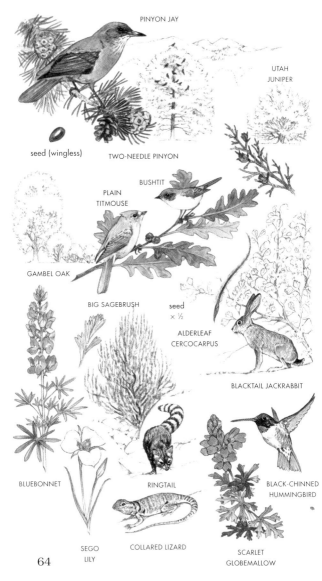

PINYON JAY

UTAH JUNIPER

seed (wingless)

TWO-NEEDLE PINYON

BUSHTIT

PLAIN TITMOUSE

GAMBEL OAK

BIG SAGEBRUSH

seed × ½

ALDERLEAF CERCOCARPUS

BLACKTAIL JACKRABBIT

BLUEBONNET

RINGTAIL

BLACK-CHINNED HUMMINGBIRD

SEGO LILY

COLLARED LIZARD

SCARLET GLOBEMALLOW

This is a desertlike "pygmy forest," made up of **Two-needle Pinyon** and several juniper species, including **Utah Juniper.** Pinyons and junipers are short and somewhat shrubby, rarely exceeding 30 feet in height. Pinyons have short, stiff needles. Junipers all have two types of foliage: scale-like leaves, often prickly, and small needles. Pinyons and junipers are often joined by **Gambel Oak,** a broad-leaved, deciduous tree.

Many colorful wildflowers, among them **Sego Lily, Scarlet Globemallow,** and **Bluebonnet** grow in the hot, rocky soils. The bright flowers attract numerous pollinators in the form of bees, butterflies, and hummingbirds, including the **Black-chinned Hummingbird.** Only the males have black chins and purple throats.

Alderleaf Cercocarpus, also called Mountain-mahogany, has seeds with long, feathery tails; the word cercocarpus means "tailed fruit." **Big Sagebrush** is one of the most abundant plants in the West, carpeting dry, hot flatlands in parts of every western state except Texas. The plant has a strong, pungent odor.

The **Pinyon Jay** is a raucous bird that roams the pines, often in flocks of 50 or more, in search of the large pinyon seeds, or pine nuts, their main food. The small, gray **Plain Titmouse** sounds a bit like a chickadee, calling a wheezy *dee-dee-dee.* Like all titmice and chickadees, this species is a hole-nester, excavating its nest site in a dead pine or juniper. **Bushtits** are closely related to titmice. They build a gourd-shaped nest made of leaves, grasses, lichens, and other material skillfully woven together with spider silk. Bushtits range throughout the West, often traveling in flocks of 30 or more.

Ringtails are nocturnal relatives of Raccoons, a fact revealed by their bushy, ringed tail. **Blacktail Jackrabbits** are big, long-eared, long-legged mammals that are frequently seen during the day.

The **Collared Lizard** is named for its black collar, easily visible when the animal is sunning on a rock. When in a hurry, this lizard can get up and run on its hind legs.

Ponderosa Pine Forest

Range: Throughout the West at middle elevations.

HEPATIC TANAGER

GRACE'S WARBLER

PONDEROSA PINE

TASSEL-EARED SQUIRREL

ROCKY MOUNTAIN JUNIPER

PYGMY NUTHATCH

WESTERN BLUEBIRD

fruit × 1

ANTELOPEBRUSH

COLORADO CHIPMUNK

CURLYCUP GUMPLANT

MOUNTAIN COTTONTAIL

DESERT BUCKBRUSH

Ponderosa Pine is the most widely distributed and probably the most abundant tree in the West. Throughout the Rocky Mountains, Ponderosa Pine is a mid-elevation species, living where dry grassland and shrubby desert yields to a cooler, moister climate. Soil is rather dry in the Ponderosa Pine Forest, with rainfall usually no more than 25 inches per year, most of it in the form of spring snow. Ponderosa Pine forests are typically open, like a park, with a ground cover of grasses and wildflowers. Fire, usually set by summer lightning, reduces litter buildup and destroys competing species, thus helping preserve the stately pine groves. Mature Ponderosa Pines can reach heights of over 150 feet.

Rocky Mountain Juniper commonly occurs with Ponderosa Pine at lower elevations. Low-elevation forests also have abundant **Antelopebrush,** a spreading shrub with yellowish flowers. At higher elevations, **Desert Buckbrush,** a thorny, spreading shrub, is more common. **Curlycup Gumplant** (Gumweed) gets its name from its sticky buds.

The **Hepatic Tanager** is common in pines from southwestern North America through Central America and on south to Argentina. **Grace's Warbler** may be found foraging for insects in the canopy, a small bird among the long pine needles. Like the Hepatic Tanager, it is a bird of southwestern pine forests, migrating to Mexico for the winter. **Western Bluebird** males have blue throats and rusty backs, field marks that separate them from the similar Eastern Bluebird where their ranges overlap in the Rockies. Bluebirds require tree cavities in which to nest, so older Ponderosa Pine forests that contain dead snags are preferred. **Pygmy Nuthatches** forage in noisy flocks; their high-pitched, excited piping helps keep the group together.

The **Tassel-eared Squirrel** is unmistakable once you get a look at its ears. The **Colorado Chipmunk** is one of 21 species of chipmunk found in the West, of which six occur somewhere within the Rockies. Nuttall's Cottontail is smaller and has much shorter ears than a jackrabbit, and has a white, puffy tail.

Rocky Mountain Aspen Grove

Range: Quaking Aspen is present to some degree in all western states; most common at middle to high elevations.

PORCUPINE

VIOLET-GREEN SWALLOW

ROCKY MOUNTAIN MAPLE

QUAKING ASPEN

RED-NAPED SAPSUCKER

CHOKECHERRY

MOUNTAIN BLUEBIRD

BROAD-TAILED HUMMINGBIRD

COLORADO COLUMBINE

ROUNDLEAF SNOWBERRY

SHOWY LOCO

SHOWY DAISY

BEAVER

Quaking Aspen is the most widely distributed tree species in North America and is abundant throughout the West. Aspens often grow in dense groves. The light yellow-green, heart-shaped leaves are attached by long stalks and shiver in the slightest breeze, making the grove look like glimmering silver. In fall, aspens turn brilliant yellow or orange. Aspens grow best after fire, and their abundance is due to periodic natural fires. **Rocky Mountain Maple** commonly grows among aspens, as either a shrub or a small, spreading tree. It has opposite, strongly toothed leaves. **Chokecherry** has white flowers on long clusters that mature into black cherries. **Roundleaf Snowberry** has pinkish, bell-like flowers that become shiny white berries.

Aspen groves admit plenty of sunlight, making them ideal habitats for wildflowers. The official state flower of Colorado, the **Colorado Columbine**, often blooms among the aspens. **Showy Daisy** has a flower head made up of a yellow disk surrounded by rays that range in color from pink and lavender to white. **Showy Loco** has a fuzzy pink flower head and delicate silvery leaves.

Many bird species live in aspen groves. The **Broad-tailed Hummingbird** feeds on the nectar of columbines and other flowers. On the smooth aspen trunks, look for the horizontal rows of holes made by **Red-naped Sapsuckers,** a Rocky Mountain species closely related to the more northern and eastern Yellow-bellied Sapsucker (page 20). **Mountain Bluebirds** nest in aspen snags, as do **Violet-green Swallows.**

Two big rodents are especially fond of aspens. Look for **Porcupines** up in the canopy and **Beavers** on the ground. Both enjoy a good meal of aspen bark, and Beavers also use aspens in building their dams and lodges. Porcupines are best known for their body armor, modified hairs called quills. The Beaver, North America's largest rodent, is historically important because the search for Beaver pelts opened the West, bringing the fur trappers who discovered the passes through the Rockies and thus prepared the way for the settlers who followed on their heels.

Rocky Mountain Lodgepole Pine Forest

Range: Middle to high elevations, from the central Rocky Mountains north and farther west.

RED CROSSBILL

WHITEBARK PINE

LODGEPOLE PINE

RED SQUIRREL

WHITE-BREASTED NUTHATCH

MARTEN

PINE GROSBEAK

KINNIKINNICK

HEARTLEAF ARNICA

WYOMING PAINTBRUSH

SNOWBRUSH

Lodgepole Pines are tall, straight trees. They grow in stands so dense that little sunlight reaches the forest floor, so understory plants are sparse. The trunks of these pines are so straight that they were indeed used as poles for lodges and tepees. Lodgepole Pine is often dependent on fire for reproduction, and the forest often shows signs of fire: charred stumps, fire-scarred trunks, ashy soil. On exposed, dry sites, **Whitebark Pine,** smaller and bushier than Lodgepole, becomes common.

Snowbrush, with sticky leaves, and **Kinnikinnick** are abundant shrubs from middle to high elevations. Kinnikinnick is a low-growing, rambling shrub with small, dark green, leathery leaves and red, pea-sized berries. Flowers, pink or white, are shaped like tiny bells.

Heartleaf Arnica looks like a big yellow daisy or sunflower with heart-shaped leaves. Several arnica species occur throughout the West. **Wyoming Paintbrush,** one of nearly 200 paintbrush species in the West, is the Wyoming state flower. Many paintbrushes are root parasites; their root systems grow into those of other plants, taking food from them.

The nasal *yank-yank* of the **White-breasted Nuthatch** is frequently heard in Lodgepole Pine Forests. Nuthatches are bark foragers, with slightly upturned bills for probing under bark. White-breasts forage by hitching head-first down the tree trunk; other birds are "up-the-tree" foragers, finding insects missed by "down-the-tree" species. The **Red Crossbill** is a nomad. It is found wherever there are abundant cones, in mountain regions of North America and as far south as Nicaragua. Crossbills climb parrotlike over cone clusters, extracting seeds. The robin-sized **Pine Grosbeak** ranges throughout northern North America, usually in spruce and fir, eating conifer and ash seeds.

The **Red Squirrel** is abundant throughout the Rockies, always in needle-leaved trees. It eats anything from insects and birds' eggs to seeds, nuts, and even fungi. The **Marten** is a 40-inch member of the weasel family that feeds principally on Red Squirrels. Martens are usually nocturnal. A pair of Martens may have a territory of up to 15 square miles.

Rocky Mountain Riverine Forest

Range: Along streams and rivers throughout the Rocky Mountains, at all elevations.

CORDILLERAN FLYCATCHER

NETLEAF HACKBERRY

NARROWLEAF COTTONWOOD

CHOKECHERRY

AMERICAN DIPPER

MOUNTAIN ALDER

MACGILLIVRAY'S WARBLER

COMMON GOOSEBERRY

YELLOW WARBLER

COW PARSNIP

WHITE CLEMATIS

TIGER SALAMANDER

Rocky Mountain Riverine Forests are typically mixtures of cottonwoods, Ashleaf Maple, Peachleaf Willow, Green Ash, Netleaf Hackberry, Water Birch, and Mountain Alder. **Narrowleaf Cottonwood** is named for its long, slender leaves with tiny teeth. **Netleaf Hackberry** leaves have netlike veins. At high elevations, thickets of **Mountain Alder** prevail. Mountain Alder grows no taller than about 30 feet and is usually smaller.

Shrubs such as **Chokecherry** and **Common Gooseberry** grow thickly along rivers. Common Gooseberry, also called Gooseberry Currant, is a spiny shrub with pinkish flowers. Its berries are sticky and are heavily eaten by birds. Deer and Elk browse the leaves. The abundance of light along riverbanks often stimulates an abundance of vines such as **White Clematis.**

Wildflowers are also abundant, including such tall species as **Cow Parsnip,** a member of the parsley family that can grow 8 feet tall. Hundreds of tiny white flowers in a flat cluster attract pollinating insects.

Riverine areas are oases for birds. Two species, **MacGillivray's Warbler** and **American Dipper,** are both riverine specialists. Singing from an alder or willow thicket, MacGillivray's Warbler is recognized by its gray hood, bright yellow breast, and split eye ring. Dippers have the remarkable ability to swim underwater, even in currents too fast for a human to stand upright. They forage entirely underwater, capturing aquatic insect larvae. Dippers prefer streams with a lot of rubble on the bottom where insects take shelter. **Yellow Warblers** are among the most widespread and common wood warblers, found throughout all of North America into northern Alaska. From the canopy of a cottonwood, you may hear a sharp, two-note bird call, something like *pit-wheep.* The bird making this sound is the nondescript, greenish brown, 5.5-inch **Cordilleran Flycatcher.**

The 13-inch **Tiger Salamander** is one of the largest salamanders in North America, the largest ever found on land. Tiger Salamanders eat earthworms, insects, other amphibians, and even an occasional mouse.

Rocky Mountain Spruce-Fir Forest

Range: Throughout the Rocky Mountains at middle to high elevations.

SUBALPINE FIR

GRAY JAY

JACOB'S LADDER

ENGLEMANN SPRUCE

RUBY-CROWNED KINGLET

GOLDEN-CROWNED KINGLET

RED-BREASTED NUTHATCH

BLUE SPRUCE

SNOWSHOE HARE (winter)

GROUSE WHORTLEBERRY

SNOWSHOE HARE (summer)

EXPLORER'S GENTIAN

Two tree species, **Engelmann Spruce** and **Subalpine Fir,** dominate high-elevation forests throughout the central and southern Rockies. The climate is cool and moist, with frost possible any month of the year. Winter snowfall is heavy, with a few snowfields remaining through much of the summer. Spruce and fir trees have the same general shape, but spruce needles are prickly, with sharp points, and fir needles are much softer (you can remember which is which because "fir" is soft). Spruce cones dangle down; fir cones are upright. **Blue Spruce,** with blue-gray needles, is common along streams and in wet meadows.

   Grouse Whortleberry is one of the most abundant understory shrubs in the Spruce-Fir Forest. It has oval leaves and bright red fruits. **Explorer's Gentian** is common along streams. The plant is about 12 inches tall, and each stem ends in a single blue flower, spotted inside with little greenish dots. **Jacob's Ladder,** also known as Sky Pilot, produces a large lavender flower with yellow anthers. Look for it at high elevations, usually between 9,000 and 12,000 feet, anywhere in the Rocky Mountains.

   Perhaps the most characteristic bird of the high Spruce-Fir Forest is the husky **Gray Jay,** sometimes called Camp Robber for its habit of boldly landing on picnic tables and helping itself. The **Red-breasted Nuthatch** is one of the most abundant northern birds. Often in company of kinglets, the nuthatch searches the conifers for insects and spiders. It often forages by hitching head-first down a trunk. The **Ruby-crowned Kinglet** and the **Golden-crowned Kinglet** can both be found throughout mountain forests. Kinglets are among the tiniest of birds, second only to hummingbirds. They flit from tree to tree, often hovering momentarily at a needle cluster or cone. The Golden-crowned Kinglet has a yellow cap, brilliant orange in males. The Ruby-crowned has a red topknot, usually concealed but visible if the bird is excited.

   The **Snowshoe Hare** ranges throughout northern North America. It turns color with the seasons; it's white in winter and mottled brown in summer.

Rocky Mountain High Pine Forest

Range: Dry, windswept sites throughout the central and southern Rocky Mountains.

CLARK'S NUTCRACKER

LIMBER PINE

BRISTLECONE PINE

SUBALPINE FIR

LEAST CHIPMUNK

SUBALPINE LARCH

COMMON JUNIPER

THREE-TOED WOODPECKER

LANCELEAF SEDUM

BUSHYTAIL WOODRAT

ROCKCRESS

In the High Pine Forest, the mountain slopes are dry and windswept, and trees rarely exceed 30 feet in height. Here you'll find the twisted, gnarled **Rocky Mountain Bristlecone Pine,** which can live as long as 2,000 years. Many have stood firm against time for 10 times as long as there has been a United States. As the centuries pass, Bristlecones tend to die slowly, losing some bark to fire and some to the appetites of Porcupines, suffering damage from wind, ice, and occasional lightning strikes. Other trees here include **Limber Pine**, with short needles in bundles of five, and **Subalpine Larch,** a deciduous conifer that drops its needles in fall. **Common Juniper** is the only juniper to grow as a shrub. Large thickets of it carpet exposed sites, forming mats up to 10 feet in diameter.

Rockcress is one of the few wildflowers able to thrive in the poor, dry soils of the high pine forest. It is an upright plant with small white flowers. **Lanceleaf Sedum,** also known as Yellow Stonecrop, is recognized by its thick, fleshy, waxy leaves, which retain moisture.

Clark's Nutcracker is a permanent resident of all western mountains. Virtually every visitor to western national parks gets to see this bird, because it often seeks handouts at places where tourists gather. It has a long bill, a gray body, and black wings and tail. Nutcrackers normally travel in small flocks, moving up and down mountain slopes in search of pine seeds, which they collect and bury, to be dug up again in winter. The **Three-toed Woodpecker** is often found in recently burned areas, where it quietly searches for bark beetles in the snags.

The **Least Chipmunk** is the smallest of the chipmunks, but has the widest geographical and altitudinal range, being equally at home on sagebrush flats, in Ponderosa Pine, among the spruces and Douglas-fir, or climbing up into a Limber Pine to get a seed or two. The **Bushytail Woodrat,** commonly called "packrat," is known for hoarding food and other objects in its middens, or large nests. Bushytail Woodrats accumulate not only sticks, nuts, mushrooms, seeds, and leaves, but also shiny objects like coins and bottle caps.

Animals of Alpine Areas

MOUNTAIN GOAT

PIKA

HOARY MARMOT

YELLOWBELLY MARMOT

Brown-capped

WHITE-TAILED PTARMIGAN

(summer)

(winter)

ROSY FINCH

Black

AMERICAN PIPIT

MOUNTAIN GOAT

Mountain Goats trot up and over the narrowest of mountain ledges. They are actually not goats but "goat-antelopes." Mountain Goats are common in the national parks of the northern Rockies and at Mt. Rainier National Park in Washington.

PIKA

Pikas spend the summer collecting plant food, which they pile into haystacks. In fall, the haystacks are taken into the Pika's den under the rocks for the winter. Pikas can be seen at many western national parks.

YELLOWBELLY MARMOT

Common on many western mountains, Yellowbellies excavate a den under a large rock or boulder that serves as a sentinel post. Should the marmot spot danger, such as a Coyote or Golden Eagle, it will stand upright, whistle loudly, and scurry into its den.

HOARY MARMOT

Hoaries are marmots of the Pacific Northwest, found in mountains into far northern Alaska, where they are animals of the arctic tundra. They are considerably larger than Yellowbelly Marmots.

WHITE-TAILED PTARMIGAN

These chickenlike birds are almost entirely white in winter, mottled brown and white in summer. This seasonal camouflage is important for a bird that spends nearly all of its time in the open. In winter, ptarmigans' feet become densely feathered, retaining heat and helping them walk on soft snow.

AMERICAN PIPIT

The 7-inch American Pipit is a tawny bird more often heard than seen, as during courtship it soars high overhead while singing its melodious song. On the ground it is well camouflaged, and it walks, not hops. Look for its white outer tail feathers.

ROSY FINCH

Rosy Finches are elegant birds of the high snowfields. Larger and huskier than sparrows, they often search for seeds and insects at the edges of melting snow. The two shown are the "Brown-capped" and the "Black," with a black head and breast.

Southwestern Arroyo and Desert Scrub

Range: From Texas west, throughout the deserts.

CRISSAL THRASHER

PHAINOPEPLA

HONEY MESQUITE

GREGG CATCLAW

BELL'S VIREO

fruit

TEXAS LIGNUMVITAE

LUCY'S WARBLER

VERDIN

BLACK-TAILED GNATCATCHER

FRENCH TAMARISK

flower × 4

scalelike leaves

TEXAS FORESTIERA

PYRRHULOXIA

An arroyo is a desert streambed that, while bone dry most of the year, can fill during intense summer rains with frightening quickness, flooding roads and surrounding areas. Water drains deep into the sandy arroyo soil, supplying trees and other plants that can reach down deeply enough to get it, such as the acacias and mesquites. **Honey Mesquite** is widely distributed throughout the Southwest and Mexico. It is often the most numerous tree of the arroyos, and typically reaches a height of about 20 feet. It has a deep taproot that can reach underground water. The common desert acacias are called "catclaws" for their curved thorns. **Gregg Catclaw** is the most widely distributed species. It often forms dense thickets that provide cover for wildlife. The odd **French Tamarisk,** commonly known as Salt-cedar, is native to Eurasia and was introduced as an ornamental and for erosion control. It has spread widely and has begun to push out native trees from arroyos throughout the Southwest. **Texas Lignumvitae** and **Texas Forestiera** are common in the Chihuahua Desert in southwest Texas and neighboring Mexico. Both have leaflets that tend to curl at the edges, which reduces water loss.

The arroyo thickets are nesting and feeding areas for many birds. Nondescript **Bell's Vireos**, hiding deep in the shade of the mesquite, sing their monotonous question, an upslurred *cheedle-cheedle-cheedle-dee?* answered with a downslurred *cheedle-cheedle-cheedle-do.* **Lucy's Warbler** is a small, active warbler. Both males and females are mostly gray with rusty orange rumps. Males also have orange on the top of their heads. **Verdins** and **Black-tailed Gnatcatchers** are also mostly gray, but male Verdins have a yellow head, and gnatcatchers are slender with a long tail. One of the most secretive birds of the arroyos, the slender **Crissal Thrasher,** can be heard in early morning, singing its melodious song from a song perch atop a mesquite. Easier to see, the colorful **Pyrrhuloxia** looks like a grayish cardinal. Mistletoe berries are heavily fed upon by the **Phainopepla,** a shiny black bird with bright red eyes and a ragged crest.

Texas/Mexican Foothill Forest

Range: Chisos Mountains in the Big Bend area of Texas and south into Mexico, at elevations of 4,400 to 8,700 feet.

GRAY-BREASTED JAY

WESTERN PIPISTREL

GRAY VIREO

MEXICAN PINYON

WEEPING JUNIPER

TEXAS MADRONE

APACHE-PLUME

GRAY OAK

RUFOUS-SIDED TOWHEE

BLACK-TAILED RATTLESNAKE

LUCIFER HUMMINGBIRD

HAVARD PENSTEMON

SCARLET BOUVARDIA

ROCK SQUIRREL

In the foothills of west Texas and much of Mexico, pinyons and junipers are joined by many oak species, most of which have small, evergreen, leathery leaves. Winters here are dry and relatively hot; summers are scorching, with thunderstorms. The woodland is generally open, with widely spaced, shrubby trees. The 112 oak species found within the Mexican Plateau include **Gray Oak,** a common evergreen species. The drooping foliage of **Weeping Juniper** makes it look permanently wilted. **Texas Madrone** has smooth, reddish bark and bright red berry clusters. **Mexican Pinyon** has needles in bundles of three, which helps distinguish it from its northern relatives. **Apache-plume** is a spreading shrub recognized by its large, five-petaled, white flowers that look like roses. **Havard Penstemon** is one of 31 penstemon species, all with trumpetlike flowers, found in the Southwest. **Scarlet Bouvardia** is a dense shrub that looks a bit like penstemon. Like penstemon, its bright red tubular flowers attract hummingbirds, such as the **Lucifer Hummingbird,** with its long, curved bill.

   Gray-breasted Jays are year-round residents, living in permanent flocks of from 6 to 24 birds. The nondescript **Gray Vireo** usually stays hidden in thick shrubbery, its warbling whistle a "voice in the scrub." The **Rufous-sided Towhee** ranges throughout North America; the western subspecies is black above with large white spots on the shoulder and back. Eastern birds lack the spots (see page 31). Towhees kick the leaf litter with both feet simultaneously, exposing seeds and insects.

   The **Western Pipistrel** is the smallest bat in the United States. Unlike most bats, it becomes active well before the sun sets, and it is not unusual for it to fly in broad daylight. The husky, all-gray **Rock Squirrel** is found throughout the Southwest, always within the pinyon-juniper woodlands. It frequents rocky slopes.

   The **Black-tailed Rattlesnake** is easy to identify because it is the only rattlesnake with an all-black tail. Give it a wide berth. There are many poisonous snakes in the Southwest, and all should be enjoyed from a respectful distance.

Southern Arizona Foothill Forest

Range: Southern Arizona, from Tucson south.

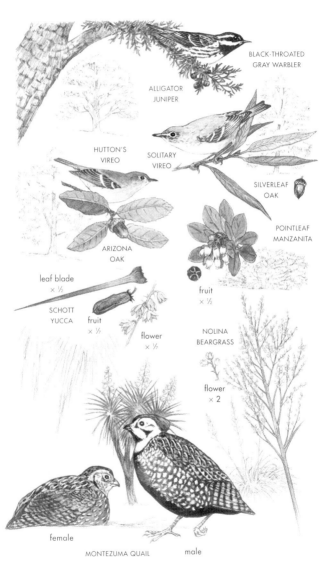

BLACK-THROATED GRAY WARBLER

ALLIGATOR JUNIPER

HUTTON'S VIREO

SOLITARY VIREO

SILVERLEAF OAK

ARIZONA OAK

POINTLEAF MANZANITA

fruit
× ½

leaf blade
× ½

SCHOTT YUCCA

fruit
× ½

flower
× ½

NOLINA BEARGRASS

flower
× 2

female

MONTEZUMA QUAIL   male

The Southern Arizona Foothill Forest, like much of northern Mexico, consists of scattered pinyons and junipers, with dense oak groves and thickets. Exposed ridges and rock faces with dry soils are inhabited by yuccas, manzanitas, and various cacti. **Alligator Juniper** has grayish black bark with a unique checkered pattern of square scales that resembles the hide of an alligator. **Arizona Oak** is recognized by its broad, oval, gray-green leaves, which tend to be hairy underneath. **Silverleaf Oak** has the narrowest leaves of any of the foothill oaks. The slender, lance-like leaves, silvery below, make the tree look like a willow.

Pointleaf Manzanita is a common evergreen shrub with smooth reddish bark and hard, brittle wood. The leathery leaves are oval, with sharp points. When a branch of the shrub touches the ground, it forms roots, eventually forming a dense, impenetrable thicket.

Yuccas are also known as Spanish bayonets or Spanish daggers. The leaves are large, stiff, sharply pointed, and often lined with spines, forming a dense cluster with a flowering stalk at the center. All have large, white flower clusters, and all are pollinated exclusively by small, white, night-flying moths, the yucca moths. Yucca moths lay their eggs in the flowers, and the caterpillars feed on yucca seeds. **Schott Yucca** is common throughout the foothills. **Nolina Beargrass** is often mistaken for a grass but is more similar to yuccas.

Dense oak thickets and open pinyon-juniper forest are ideal habitats for birds, including the grayish form of **Solitary Vireo** and the kinglet-like **Hutton's Vireo.** The distinctive **Black-throated Gray Warbler** is usually seen gleaning insects from pinyons and junipers. A walk along a grassy hillside may disturb a covey of chunky **Montezuma Quail.** These quail rarely fly, preferring to scurry away in the underbrush.

Mammals are also abundant, especially rodents. Apache Fox Squirrels perambulate through the trees, while Rock Squirrels and Cliff Chipmunks stay mostly on the ground. Black-tailed Jackrabbits and small herds of Collared Peccaries are common. Lizards and snakes can be readily found sunning on rocks.

Arizona Canyon Forest

Range: Southeastern Arizona among the Chiricahua, Huachuca, and Santa Rita Mountains.

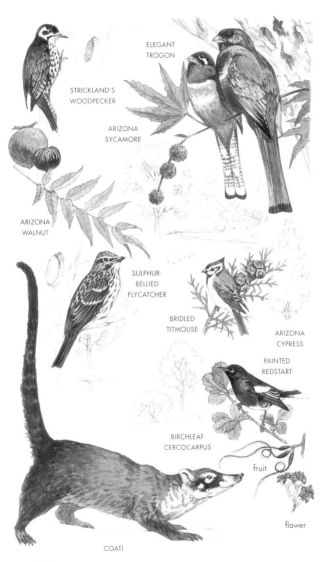

STRICKLAND'S
WOODPECKER

ELEGANT
TROGON

ARIZONA
SYCAMORE

ARIZONA
WALNUT

SULPHUR-
BELLIED
FLYCATCHER

BRIDLED
TITMOUSE

ARIZONA
CYPRESS

PAINTED
REDSTART

BIRCHLEAF
CERCOCARPUS

fruit

flower

COATI

Once the home of the Apache tribe, the steep, splendid cliffs of the southern Arizona mountains provide protection for lush canyon forests. The beautiful **Arizona Sycamore** is joined here by **Arizona Walnut** and **Arizona Cypress.** Sycamores, which line stream and riverbeds, are unmistakable, with their white bark and peeling brown flakes. Many birds and mammals use Arizona Sycamore for nesting sites. For instance, four of the five bird species shown at left (Strickland's Woodpecker, Elegant Trogon, Bridled Titmouse, and Sulfur-bellied Flycatcher) nest in cavities, usually in a sycamore. Sycamore fruits, sometimes called "buttonballs," hang in clusters of three to five per stalk. Arizona Walnut fruits are large, green balls with a hard-shelled, edible nut inside. Arizona Cypress is easy to identify because of its conical or rounded crown and scale-like, blue-green leaves.

   Birchleaf Cercocarpus (Mountain-mahogany) is one of several evergreen shrubs that are common from canyons to mountain forests in the Southwest. Though normally a spreading shrub, it can grow as tall as 25 feet.

   Canyon forests are where birders search for the brilliant **Elegant Trogon,** the equally striking **Painted Redstart**, the noisy and conspicuous **Sulfur-bellied Flycatcher,** the quiet **Strickland's Woodpecker,** and flocks of noisy **Bridled Timice.** The trogon and the flycatcher, both Mexican species, are found only in sycamore canyons. At first glance, the male Elegant Trogon looks rather parrotlike. It is deep iridescent green, with a bright red breast and orangy upper tail. The Painted Redstart is sometimes called *mariposa,* which means butterfly in Spanish. It forages with its wings and tail spread, seeming to flit erratically, almost bouncing from tree trunk to branch like a feathered butterfly.

   The **Coati,** sometimes called Coati Mundi, is a sleek, tropical member of the raccoon family. It is rarely alone; bands of up to two dozen Coatis roam the woods, usually at night, in search of anything from insects and lizards to prickly-pears and manzanita fruits.

Southwestern Mountain Forest

Range: Southern New Mexico and southern Arizona.

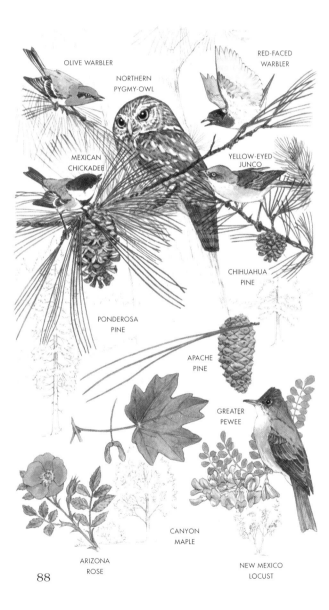

OLIVE WARBLER

RED-FACED WARBLER

NORTHERN PYGMY-OWL

MEXICAN CHICKADEE

YELLOW-EYED JUNCO

CHIHUAHUA PINE

PONDEROSA PINE

APACHE PINE

GREATER PEWEE

CANYON MAPLE

ARIZONA ROSE

NEW MEXICO LOCUST

Southwestern Mountain Forests have many Mexican pine species, including **Chihuahua Pine** and **Apache Pine,** as well as a unique variety of **Ponderosa Pine** with needles in bundles of 5 rather than the usual 3. The forest is often open and parklike, with a soft litter of fallen pine needles. The fragrant odor of pine resin permeates the air. Apache Pine needles may be up to 15 inches long, longer and darker than those of Ponderosa Pine. Chihuahua Pine is a small, rugged tree that lives at high elevations. It has blue-green needles, 2–4 inches in length, in bundles of 3. Shrubs and small trees include manzanitas, buckthorns, gooseberries, **Arizona Rose,** and **New Mexico Locust.** Arizona Rose is a colorful shrub found only in Arizona. New Mexico Locust is recognized by its delicate compound leaves and pink flower clusters. Along streamsides, **Canyon Maple,** also called Bigtooth Maple because of the deep lobes of its leaves, is common.

Like the trees, some of the bird species are also primarily Mexican, occurring nowhere else in the United States but in these forests. These species include the colorful **Red-faced Warbler, Olive Warbler, Mexican Chickadee, Yellow-eyed Junco,** and **Greater Pewee.** These species often forage together in mixed flocks, searching the forest for food. The pewee is usually at the treetop, waiting to fly out and snatch an airborne insect. The junco tends to stay on the forest floor, searching the litter for insects and plant food. The chickadees and warblers are active, flitting about the branches and searching needles, bark, and cones for food. The **Northern Pygmy-owl** is a common but infrequently seen small owl of all western forests. As the plate shows, a Northern Pygmy-owl can easily attract a crowd. Small birds are apt to "mob" a predator discovered in their midst. Though pygmy-owls hunt mostly rodents, small birds such as warblers and chickadees nonetheless seem to regard them as a potential danger.

The Apache Fox Squirrel and the Cliff Chipmunk are the two most frequently sighted mammals of the Southwest Mountain Forest.

Sonoran Desert Giant Cactus Forest

Range: Southern Arizona and extreme south-eastern California into Mexico.

OCOTILLO

ELF OWL

flower ×1

leaves ×3

CREOSOTE BUSH

SAGUARO

GILA WOODPECKER

ENGELMANN'S PRICKLY-PEAR

YUMA ANTELOPE SQUIRREL

CACTUS WREN

CHAIN CHOLLA

GILA MONSTER

GREATER ROADRUNNER

The giant **Saguaro** cactus (pronounced *sah-WAH-roe*) dominates gentle slopes, called *bajadas*, throughout much of the hot, dry Sonoran Desert. Many people don't think of the desert as a forest habitat, but the Saguaro often grows to tree size, up to 50 feet and occasionally taller. The accordian pleats of its spiny stems allow the plant to soak up water and store it. The weight of a mature Saguaro (up to 7 tons) can be 95% water. Many other cactuses are present in the Giant Cactus Forest, and some are incredibly spiny, so walk carefully. The chollas (pronounced *CHOY-ah*) are extremely spiny, and the joints break off and stick to skin and clothing so readily that it is often called "jumping cholla." **Chain Cholla,** a densely branched, shrubby cactus, grows to about 10 feet tall. **Engelmann's Prickly-pear** is a common cactus eaten by peccaries, cottontails, and Desert Tortoises.

Ocotillo, which is not a cactus, resembles a cluster of gray-green buggy whips. For most of the year the plant is leafless, which reduces water loss. It grows tiny leaves after it rains. Ocotillo flowers in spring, when hummingbirds are migrating; up to six species help pollinate the bright red flower clusters. **Creosote Bush** is a multi-stemmed shrub, identified by its strong odor and tiny paired leaves, pointed at the ends. Creosote Bush lives where Saguaros cannot, on the flat plains in scorching heat.

The **Greater Roadrunner** can be seen running along desert roads in pursuit of invertebrates as well as an array of lizards, mice, and even other birds. The **Elf Owl** is the world's smallest owl, a sparrow-sized bird that nests in Saguaros. The Elf Owl probably owes its desert home to the work of a **Gila Woodpecker.** The cavities it excavates in the giant cactuses are widely used by other species. **Cactus Wrens,** the largest of North American wrens, frequently nest in chollas. Cactus Wrens forage in noisy family groups.

The **Gila Monster** is the only poisonous lizard in the United States. They hunt mice, birds, and other lizards. They have powerful jaws with which they hold their prey firmly, injecting poison from glands in their lower jaws.

Sierra Nevada Pine Forests

Range: Low to middle elevations throughout the Sierra Nevada of California.

BROWN
CREEPER

JEFFREY PINE

PONDEROSA
PINE

WESTERN
WOOD-PEWEE

COOPER'S HAWK

CALIFORNIA
BLACK OAK

WESTERN
SCREECH-OWL

GREENLEAF
MANZANITA

KIT-KIT-DIZZE

pod

GOLDEN-MANTLED
SQUIRREL

WALLFLOWER

Sierra Nevada is Spanish for "snow range." At middle elevations in this California mountain range, **Ponderosa Pine** is abundant. It is joined by and sometimes hybridizes with a very similar species, **Jeffrey Pine,** which is almost entirely confined to this area. Ponderosa Pine predominates on the west side of the Sierra, where it mixes with other species. Jeffrey Pine replaces Ponderosa at higher elevations and on the eastern side of the Sierra. Jeffrey Pine cones are longer than Ponderosa's and feel much less prickly. **California Black Oak** is immediately identified by its large, deeply lobed leaves with sharp points at the tips. The leaves turn yellow to golden brown in autumn. **Greenleaf Manzanita** is most abundant on recently burned areas. It has smooth, leathery, dark green leaves, and its multiple stems are deep reddish, with smooth bark. **Kit-kit-dizze,** also called Mountain Misery, is a low, spreading shrub with fernlike, evergreen leaves that are densely hairy and sticky. The plant has a pungent odor. **Wallflower** is common in open areas with lots of sunlight and is often seen at the roadside. Flowers are usually yellow but may be deep orange.

Four widespread western birds are common in the Sierra Nevada Pine Forests. The **Western Screech-Owl** sings a series of monotonous softly whistled notes that run together at the end, a song that has been compared to a bouncing ball coming to a stop. **Cooper's Hawks** prey almost exclusively on birds, remaining motionless and quiet in the canopy, suddenly darting through the forest to strike down its unsuspecting prey. The unmusical call of the **Western Wood-Pewee,** a dry *pweeer,* is sometimes the only bird sound in a western forest during the hottest part of the day. The **Brown Creeper** feeds by landing near the base of the tree trunk and methodically spiraling its way upward, removing insects from the bark with its thin, curved bill.

The **Golden-mantled Squirrel** has bright orangy cheeks and an unstriped face, distinguishing it from chipmunks. It carries food in its bulging cheek pouches, returning to its underground den to add to its winter larder.

Giant Sequoia Grove

Range: The west side of the Sierra Nevada range, mostly between 5,000 and 7,000 feet in elevation.

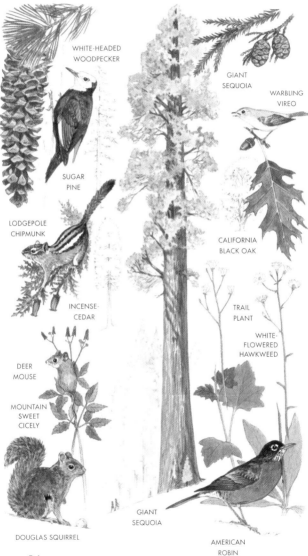

WHITE-HEADED WOODPECKER

GIANT SEQUOIA

WARBLING VIREO

SUGAR PINE

LODGEPOLE CHIPMUNK

CALIFORNIA BLACK OAK

INCENSE-CEDAR

TRAIL PLANT

WHITE-FLOWERED HAWKWEED

DEER MOUSE

MOUNTAIN SWEET CICELY

DOUGLAS SQUIRREL

GIANT SEQUOIA

AMERICAN ROBIN

Giant Sequoia, once widespread, survives today only in 75 scattered groves on the western side of the Sierra Nevada. They stand tall and bulky, with tight crowns and wide trunks, the deep reddish bark thick and furrowed, often scarred by fire. The adult trees are the largest organisms on the planet: a Giant Sequoia averages about 250 feet tall, with a diameter of 10 to 15 feet. The tree called "General Sherman" at Sequoia National Park is 36.5 feet thick at its base and weighs 12 million pounds! Giant Sequoias, like many other western trees, require periodic natural fires to maintain healthy groves. Fire prepares the seedbed by burning litter and exposing bare soil. Updrafts from ground fires cause the closed cones to open, releasing seeds. After ground fires, there are thousands of Sequoia seedlings per acre. Fire also burns away competing trees that would eventually replace the Sequoias. The thick bark of mature Sequoias is highly fire-resistant.

Sugar Pine, the largest North American pine, routinely tops 200 feet. Its cones, up to 20 inches long, are the longest of any pine in North America. **Incense-cedar,** which occurs widely throughout the Sierra Nevada, has scale-like needles that are aromatic when crushed.

Several wildflowers add color to the Sequoia groves, including **Mountain Sweet Cicely, Trail Plant,** and **White-flowered Hawkweed.**

Giant Sequoia groves are so overwhelming that animals seem swallowed up by the living wood. A **White-headed Woodpecker** looks tiny when hitching up the enormous trunks. The persistent song of the plain-colored **Warbling Vireo** can be heard in Sequoia groves, but the singer can be very tricky to find, as it tends to move slowly through the dense foliage. On the ground, however, **American Robins,** ubiquitous throughout North America, seek worms.

The **Douglas Squirrel,** also called Chickaree, is familiar to most visitors of Pacific Coast forests. The **Lodgepole Chipmunk** occurs only in central California and is one of two chipmunk species in the Sequoia groves. The **Deer Mouse** is abundant in forests and prairies throughout the West, from Alaska to Mexico.

Sierra Conifer Forests

Range: Sierra Nevada mountains at elevations of about 4,000 to 9,000 feet.

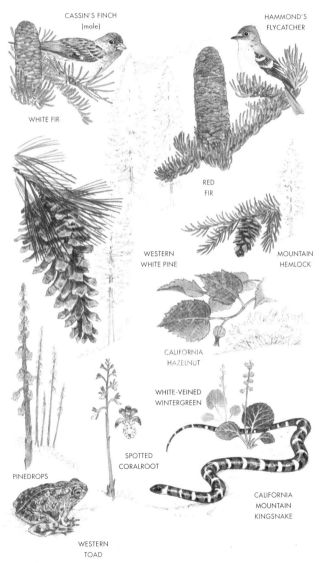

CASSIN'S FINCH
(male)

HAMMOND'S
FLYCATCHER

WHITE FIR

RED
FIR

WESTERN
WHITE PINE

MOUNTAIN
HEMLOCK

CALIFORNIA
HAZELNUT

WHITE-VEINED
WINTERGREEN

SPOTTED
CORALROOT

PINEDROPS

CALIFORNIA
MOUNTAIN
KINGSNAKE

WESTERN
TOAD

Conifers, especially **White Fir** and **Red Fir,** are abundant in the Sierra. White Fir is generally found at lower elevations on the western slopes, whereas Red Fir can be found on either side of the Sierra, usually at higher elevations where snow can persist through June. White Fir is identified by its pale, soft, twisted needles. Red Fir is named for its bark, which is deep reddish brown and furrowed. Its needles are distinctly curved and four-sided. Other trees of the high-elevation "snowbelt" are **Western White Pine,** with needles in bundles of 5 and limbs that tend to curve gently upward; and **Mountain Hemlock,** a picturesque tree sometimes exceeding 100 feet. Its feathery branches and spire droop, a useful field mark for identifying the species at a distance.

California Hazelnut, a broad-leaved, deciduous tree, is found in mountains and northern regions throughout North America. Its fruits have distinctive brown husks with fibrous "beaks." The nuts are an important food for wildlife, as are the twigs and leaves.

Pinedrops grows as a cluster of fuzzy pink stems with little bell-like flowers. The plant lacks leaves; it survives in deep shade because its root system grows in decomposing litter to obtain its food, much like a fungus. **Spotted Coralroot** is an elegant little orchid common in the shade of the fir forests.

Cassin's Finch, a sparrow-sized, reddish bird, is apt to be seen singing its warbling song atop a fir spire. **Hammond's Flycatcher,** a plain little bird, often flicks its wings, giving it a nervous look. Its call is a demonstrative, unmusical *zwe-beek!*

The **California Mountain Kingsnake** is banded in red, black, and white, with each red band touching two black bands. It is a predator, feeding mostly on mice and moles. The **Western Toad** is common throughout the Pacific Northwest and California. Toads live on the forest floor, usually beneath a rock or log during the day. Their mating call, heard when they return to water to mate in spring, has been compared with the piping of goslings. The small, black tadpoles can be found in mountain ponds through August.

Sierra Nevada Subalpine Forest

Range: Higher elevations throughout the Sierra Nevada. Ancient Great Basin Bristlecone Pines can be seen at Inyo National Forest near Bishop, Calif.

GREAT GRAY OWL

GREAT BASIN BRISTLECONE PINE

FOXTAIL PINE

SWAINSON'S THRUSH

WESTERN JUNIPER

HUCKLEBERRY OAK

SIERRA PRIMROSE

COMB DRABA

BUSH CHINKAPIN

HERMIT THRUSH

PINEMAT MANZANITA

APLODONTIA

The Sierra Nevada Subalpine Forest is a rugged, open, timberline forest. The scenery is spectacular: stunted, gnarled trees, wildflower and sedge meadows, and geologic oddities such as granite outcrops and talus slopes. Winters are long and cold, and the wind chill is intense. Most of the hardy trees found here are pines, notably the **Great Basin Bristlecone Pine.** This tree has been known to live 4,600 years; some individuals are the oldest single organisms on Earth. It occurs on scattered peaks in the Great Basin east of the Sierra. The cones are covered with prickles. **Foxtail Pine** and the similar Whitebark Pine, like Bristlecone, have short, dark green needles in bundles of 5. Foxtail needle bundles lie in dense clumps close against the branches, giving the branch a bushy "foxtail." Mountain Hemlock and **Western Juniper** also are found here. Western Juniper has a thick, twisted, vivid reddish trunk.

Shrubs here include **Bush Chinkapin,** whose leaves are yellow-gold below, giving the shrub its alternate name, Golden Chinkapin. **Huckleberry Oak** is a shrub oak, the only source of acorns for the several chipmunk and ground squirrel species found at higher elevations. **Pinemat Manzanita** spreads over bare ground or granite rock faces. Its peeling bark is smooth and reddish.

Sierra Primrose is a creeping wildflower, its flat leaf clusters tightly hugging rock faces, where they can absorb maximum sunlight in the short growing season. **Comb Draba,** with tiny yellow flowers, grows in crevices between rocks, spreading over rock faces.

A glimpse of the **Great Gray Owl** is a thrill for birders in the Sierra. These big predators commonly hunt in the subalpine areas, especially meadows. They often nest in an old hawk nest. The **Hermit Thrush** and **Swainson's Thrush** are both common throughout western mountains. Both have fluting, melodious songs, usually sung at dusk and dawn. Swainson's Thrush has a buffy eye ring and buffy cheeks. The Hermit Thrush has a rusty tail.

The **Aplodontia** is a rarely observed mammal that lives along streams at all elevations. It gnaws bark, in a manner similar to Porcupines.

California Oak-Pine Woodland

Range: West of the Sierra, at elevations from 300 to 5,000 feet.

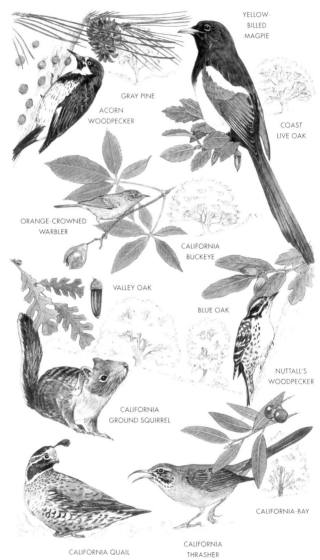

YELLOW-BILLED MAGPIE

GRAY PINE

ACORN WOODPECKER

COAST LIVE OAK

ORANGE-CROWNED WARBLER

CALIFORNIA BUCKEYE

VALLEY OAK

BLUE OAK

NUTTALL'S WOODPECKER

CALIFORNIA GROUND SQUIRREL

CALIFORNIA-BAY

CALIFORNIA QUAIL

CALIFORNIA THRASHER

The foothill Oak-Pine Woodlands of California are composed of many oak species, plus **California-bay, California Buckeye,** and **Gray Pine.** The gentle hillsides, covered by tall, golden yellow grasses and dotted with rounded, symmetrical trees, are among the most beautiful habitats in California.

California has nine species of tree-sized oaks and 12 shrub oaks. **Valley Oak** is a deciduous oak, with small leaves that have deeply rounded lobes. **Coast Live Oak** has hollylike, curved leaves, usually with sharp spines along the margins. The leaves feel leathery and thick, a characteristic of the evergreen oaks. **Blue Oak** is deciduous, with elliptical, pale blue-green leaves, smooth along the margins. It grows where conditions are dry and hot. Gray Pine, also called Digger Pine, has long (7–14 inches), drooping, gray-green needles, in bundles of 3. The cones are rounded and prickly. California-bay, also called Laurel, has evergreen leaves with a strong, pungent odor. California Buckeye leaves have five leaflets radiating from a common base. In spring, it is covered with clusters of pink blossoms.

The Oak-Pine Woodland is rich with animals, especially birds. The gaudy, noisy **Acorn Woodpeckers** live in groups that store hundreds of acorns in tree trunks. **Nuttall's Woodpecker,** which occurs only in these woodlands, can be found probing bark. The large and easily identified **Yellow-billed Magpie** is also entirely confined to a small area within the oak woodlands. **California Quail** are common in the understory. The **California Thrasher** normally stays pretty much out of sight, though a male will sing from atop an open song perch. It commonly mimics other birds.

Two sizable rodents, the **California Ground Squirrel** and Western Gray Squirrel (page 112), are common, the former living in burrows on the ground, the latter scampering about in the branches above. Other mammals, including jackrabbits, Raccoons, and Striped Skunks, are commonly seen, and Mule Deer are abundant in many places. Even predators such as Gray Foxes and Bobcats are seen fairly frequently.

California Chaparral

Range: Throughout the foothills of central and southern California.

CHAMISE

WHITELEAF
MANZANITA

GOPHER
SNAKE

TOYON

SCRUB JAY

COMMON
BUCKBRUSH

CALIFORNIA
TOWEE

CALIFORNIA
SCRUB OAK

WRENTIT

CALIFORNIA
POPPY

CHAPARRAL
PEA

BEWICK'S
WREN

COAST HORNED
LIZARD

Chaparral, from the Spanish for scrub oak, is a community of tough, fire-adapted shrubs, usually growing in dense thickets in areas with wet, mild winters and hot, dry summers. Fire, usually set by lightning in the summer dry season, is common. Chaparral shrubs quickly recolonize after a burn.

Though chaparral looks monotonous, more than 900 plant species have been found here. The shrubs all have leathery, stiff, waxy leaves. Some, such as **Chamise, Whiteleaf Manzanita,** and **Common Buckbrush,** are extremely widespread. Chamise has needlelike leaves growing in clusters from points along the stems and spikes of small, white flowers. Whiteleaf Manzanita has shiny, reddish bark that peels in thin strips. Common Buckbrush is one of many North American wild lilacs. Its small, oval leaves resemble sagebrush leaves.

California Scrub Oak is a spreading shrub with small, spiny leaves. It is an abundant acorn producer and an important food source for chaparral animals. **Toyon,** sometimes called California Holly, has hollylike leaves, though they are not prickly. **Chaparral Pea** is a spiny shrub with large, pinkish purple flowers. Fruits are small, flat pods. **California Poppy,** the state flower of California, is often abundant on grassy areas throughout the state.

The perky, 6-inch **Wrentit** sings its distinctive song at any time of day, a series of strident notes ending in a descending trill. The **California Towhee** is brown, with a rusty throat and rusty below the tail. Its dry, metallic *chink* note reveals its presence in the scrub. The **Scrub Jay** is a permanent resident throughout much of the West. It is a blue, crestless jay that typically flies in small, often extremely noisy flocks, communicating with a dry, harsh *kweeah.* **Bewick's Wren** is common in backyards and thickets in much of the West. It is an active, noisy bird with a white eye stripe and zebra stripes on its outer tail feathers.

Rodents are abundant in chaparral, attracting predators such as Bobcat, Coyote, and the widespread **Gopher Snake.** The local **Coast Horned Lizard** has numerous spines to protect it from predators. It eats ants.

California Coastal Forest and Scrub

Range: Coastal California, north to southern Oregon.

MONTEREY
PINE

MONARCH

MONTEREY
CYPRESS

GOLDEN-CROWNED
SPARROW

COYOTE
BUSH

BUSH
LUPINE

BLACK
SAGE

MONTEREY
PAINTBRUSH

POISON-OAK

LESSER
GOLDFINCH

BRUSH RABBIT

The Coastal Forest of California features wave-splashed dunes, moorlike scrub, picturesque pine forests, and stately Douglas-fir and Redwood groves. Several coastal tree species occur nowhere else, including **Monterey Cypress,** a wind-sculpted, flat-topped evergreen found only in two groves near Monterey and Carmel. Several pine species, including **Monterey Pine,** Torrey Pine, and Bishop Pine, are entirely restricted to narrow coastal areas. The cones on these pines remain closed on the tree until fire or age causes them to drop off and open.

Exposed coastal areas support desertlike shrub communities called coastal scrub, dominated by **Coyote Bush, Black Sage, Bush Lupine, Poison-oak,** and others, as well as various grasses and many wildflowers. Coyote Bush is a stiff shrub with leathery leaves. In late summer and fall, its seeds are released on feathery parachutes. Bush Lupine, covered in spring with spikes of bright yellow flowers, adds brilliant color to the coastal scrub. Seeds are in dry, brown pods that hang loosely atop the shrub. Poison-oak is recognized by its three leaflets, each gently lobed. It is not a true oak but a close relative of Poison-ivy, and it produces similar skin irritations if touched. Black Sage is most common in southern California. Like other sages, it is aromatic. **Monterey Paintbrush** is one of dozens of colorful wildflowers found among the coastal scrub.

As caterpillars, **Monarch** butterflies feed exclusively on milkweeds, later becoming one of the brightest and largest of our butterflies. Protected from birds by the poisons they acquire from milkweed, their bright orange color is an example of warning coloration.

Golden-crowned Sparrows, which nest in Canada and Alaska, winter in California. Flocks of these large, attractive sparrows can be found feeding on seeds of shrubs and wildflowers. Bright yellow **Lesser Goldfinches,** also seed-eaters, are year-round residents of coastal scrub as well as thickets and woodlands throughout the Southwest.

Skulking in the shade of the coastal scrub, the **Brush Rabbit** is identified by its compact shape, small tail, and short, dark ears.

California Riverine Forest

Range: Throughout California.

BELTED KINGFISHER

BLACK PHOEBE

BONPLAND WILLOW

CALIFORNIA SYCAMORE

WOOD DUCK

BLUE ELDERBERRY

FREMONT COTTONWOOD

LAZULI BUNTING

WHITE ALDER

SPOTTED SANDPIPER

STREAM ORCHID

CALIFORNIA NEWT

YELLOW MONKEY-FLOWER

California's rivers and streams are lined with lush forests, providing ideal habitat for animals. The **California Sycamore** has light brown outer bark that peels away, exposing smooth white inner bark below. Its leaves are star-shaped and fruits are dry balls. **Fremont Cottonwood** typically has a wide trunk with thick, spreading branches and corky, deep-furrowed bark. **Bonpland Willow** is one of many North American willow species that occur along streams and rivers. Bonpland Willow leaves are pale green above (all other willows are darker green) and silvery and often hairy below. **White Alder** grows in dense thickets along mountain streams. It is identified by its fine-toothed leaves and conelike catkins.

Blue Elderberry is a shrub or small tree with white flowers clustered in broad, flat sprays. The fruits are dark blue berries. **Yellow Monkeyflower** is a bright yellow, trumpet-shaped flower that grows in bushy clumps up to 3 feet high, usually along streams. **Stream Orchid** is a tall, elegant plant found along streams from Mexico through British Columbia.

Listen for the loud rattling call of the **Belted Kingfisher.** Kingfishers dive for fish and nest in tunnels dug in streambanks. The colorful **Wood Duck** nests in hollow trees, sometimes far from the water's edge. Wood Ducks will suddenly fly up from the water, loudly calling *week-week!* as they disappear in the woods. Walking and teetering along the pebbles and rocks that line a river, bobbing its tail constantly, the unobtrusive **Spotted Sandpiper** probes the gravel for insects and other morsels. The **Black Phoebe** doesn't teeter, but it, too, bobs its tail. This little black flycatcher with a white belly is typically observed perched in the open on a low branch as it waits for a flying insect to come within range. The **Lazuli Bunting** is a bird of brushy areas. Males are easy to identify, being lazuli blue above and rusty on the breast, with two distinct white wing bars.

The **California Newt** is blackish above and buffy yellow below, with bumpy, warty skin. It is common along streams throughout most of coastal California as well as much of the Sierra.

Redwood Forest

Range: From extreme southwestern Oregon along the coast to central California.

REDWOOD

WESTERN HEMLOCK

PACIFIC RHODODENDRON

BLUEBLOSSOM CEANOTHUS

WESTERN AZALEA

EVERGREEN HUCKLEBERRY

ANNA'S HUMMINGBIRD

FIVE-FINGERED FERN

SINGLE SUGAR SCOOP

WILSON'S WARBLER

REDWOOD

REDWOOD SORREL

Although the Sequoia is more massive, the **Redwood** is the tallest tree on Earth. It routinely reaches heights of 300 feet, and some are as tall as 350 feet. The trunk is usually ramrod straight, with no divisions. Long branches covered with dark green needles spray out, the lower branches drooping. The bark is deep reddish, with thick furrows and loose fibers. Many trees have huge, warty growths on their trunks called burls. Burls may sprout new stems if the tree is damaged. Redwoods require lots of moisture, which they get by "combing" water droplets out of the fog brought in by the cool waters of the Pacific Ocean. Redwood seedlings grow rapidly in recently burned soils. Mature trees are protected from fire to a large extent by their thick bark.

Redwood forests typically have a well-developed understory, including **Pacific Rhododendron** and **Western Azalea.** These two colorful shrubs bloom in spring and early summer. Other shrubs, including **Evergreen Huckleberry** and **Blueblossom Ceanothus,** are usually present. Many ferns grow in the cool shade, including the distinctive **Five-fingered Fern. Redwood Sorrel,** a wildflower with cloverlike leaves, forms a natural carpet. **Single Sugar Scoop** is one of several tall wildflowers found among the Redwoods. Flowers are tiny and white, dangling bell-like from stalks.

Redwoods mix with **Western Hemlocks,** Grand Fir, Western Redcedar, and others. Western Hemlock, at first glance, looks much like Redwood, but its needles vary in size, whereas Redwood needles are all the same size.

Among the world's tallest trees can be found one of the world's smallest birds, the **Anna's Hummingbird.** The male is emerald green with iridescent rosy red on its throat and forehead. **Wilson's Warbler** is a small, black-capped wood warbler. Look for it skulking among the understory shrubs, especially along streams. Many other animals live in the Redwood Forest, including the Spotted Owl, both Douglas and Western Gray Squirrels, and two chipmunk species. Mule Deer are commonly seen at Redwood National Park, and Elk can sometimes be spotted as well.

Northwest Oak-Pine Forest

Range: Throughout the Pacific Northwest to northern California.

DUSKY FLYCATCHER

OREGON WHITE OAK

KNOBCONE PINE

GREAT HORNED OWL

PACIFIC MADRONE

HARDHACK

COMMON CAMAS

WESTERN LARKSPUR

NORTHWESTERN GARTER SNAKE

MOUNTAIN QUAIL

WESTERN SKINK

WHITE FAWN-LILY

FAREWELL-TO-SPRING

The Northwest Oak-Pine Forest, located on hot, dry sites, consists of small, rounded, picturesque trees scattered over hillsides covered with grasses and wildflowers. **Oregon White Oak,** often called Garry Oak, ranges widely through the region. It is identified by the smoothly rounded lobes of its leaves. **Pacific Madrone** is unmistakable, with bright reddish, peeling bark and leathery, evergreen leaves. **Knobcone Pine** has curved cones that are distinctly knobby on one side. The cones stay on the trunk and large branches, even becoming embedded in the tree as it grows.

Many wildflowers grow here. **Western Larkspur** often carpets the landscape, as does the shrubby **Hardhack. Common Camas** could at first easily be mistaken for a tall grass, but the deep violet flowers reveal it as a member of the lily family. **Farewell-to-Spring** acquired its odd name because its flowers, which attract bees, butterflies, and hummingbirds, bloom from late June through August. When this wildflower blooms, bid "farewell to spring" (it is also called Herald-of-Summer). **White Fawn-lilies** start to bloom earlier and continue through midsummer. The whitish flowers are pollinated mostly by bumblebees.

Many birds live in the Oak-Pine Forest. The **Great Horned Owl,** by weight the largest of the American owls, feeds on anything from mice and squirrels to grouse, ducks, and even feral cats. It is common throughout North America. The drab **Dusky Flycatcher** frequents open woodlands and scrubby habitats from northwestern Canada south to New Mexico and California. **Mountain Quail** live in dry mountain areas from Washington south through California and parts of Nevada. They migrate on foot, breeding along high slopes and wintering in more protected valleys.

The **Northwestern Garter Snake** is a handsome and harmless snake, dark above and yellow below with an orange or red stripe. More potentially dangerous but less common, the Northern Pacific Rattlesnake has dark blotches and a dark mark through its face and eye. The slender, sleek **Western Skink** is a common lizard throughout the far West.

Temperate Rain Forest 1
(see also page 114)

Range: Along the coast from Alaska through Oregon.

SITKA SPRUCE

WESTERN HEMLOCK

WESTERN REDCEDAR

WESTERN LARCH

FOX SPARROW

VARIED THRUSH

PILEATED WOODPECKER

WESTERN SWORD FERN

RUFFED GROUSE

OLD MAN'S BEARD

YELLOW PINE CHIPMUNK

WESTERN GRAY SQUIRREL

PACIFIC TREEFROG

DEVIL'S-CLUB

The Temperate Rain Forest, with abundant moisture from coastal fog, rain, and some snow, supports immensely tall trees sometimes exceeding 200 feet. Many of the trees are heavily laden with air plants such as **Old Man's Beard.** On the forest floor, lush ferns such as **Western Sword Fern** abound. The damp, mossy surfaces of fallen, decomposing logs (called nurse logs) provide habitat for scores of seedling and sapling conifers.

Sitka Spruce is a tall coastal species with very prickly needles. **Western Redcedar** has scalelike, often yellowish foliage that hangs in sprays from the tree, and reddish bark that usually peels in long strips. **Western Hemlock** has flattened needles of varying lengths. Its topmost spire droops, and its branches radiate out in flat sprays. Tiny cone clusters hang on branch tips. **Western Larch,** a fast-growing tree, is generally fire-resistant, and vast numbers of wind-blown seeds sprout on newly burned land. Its needles turn yellow and drop off the tree in late autumn. **Silver Fir,** with smooth, silvery bark, is often abundant, particularly in regions of British Columbia and the Cascade Mountains. The barrel-shaped, upright cones have a purplish tinge. **Grand Fir** needles are of two lengths and lie flat on the branches. **Pacific Yew** is normally an understory conifer, never very abundant but of great interest because of a chemical, taxol, in its bark. Taxol may be effective in retarding several kinds of cancer and so is in great demand. The seeds are contained in fleshy red "berries."

Pacific Dogwood, Vine Maple, and **Snowberry** are common in the understory. **Devil's-club** is an unmistakable shrub with long sharp thorns lining both its stems and its huge, maple-like leaves. Fruits are bright red berries. Among the wildflowers, you should find **Western Trillium,** an elegant wildflower with a single, three-petaled flower that starts out white and gradually turns red. The plant blooms in early spring. **Snow Plant** is an odd member of the wintergreen family. The bright red flowers often poke through the snow. It gets nutrition from the decomposing plants of the forest floor.

The crow-sized **Pileated Woodpecker** is

TOWNSEND'S WARBLER

CHESTNUT-BACKED CHICKADEE

SILVER FIR

GRAND FIR

PACIFIC YEW

WINTER WREN

VINE MAPLE

PACIFIC DOGWOOD

WESTERN TRILLIUM

SNOWBERRY

TOWNSEND CHIPMUNK

SNOW PLANT

ENSATINA

NORTHERN ALLIGATOR LIZARD

mostly black but reveals large white underwing patches in flight. Its carvings, large holes always oval in shape, can be found throughout the forest on dead snags and on fallen logs. The cavities eventually serve as nest sites for many other hole-nesters, both birds and mammals. **Ruffed Grouse** are birds of the forest floor, the males using logs as drumming stations on which they beat their wings during courtship. One of the most haunting sounds of the Temperate Rain Forest is the song of the **Varied Thrush,** a two-noted song of sustained minor chords. The bird has a dark band across its orange breast and an orange line extending from the back of the eye to the neck. **Fox Sparrows** are birds of the understory and ground. The presence of a Fox Sparrow is often announced by its call, a loud smacking sound. The 5-inch **Chestnut-backed Chickadee** ranges from southern Alaska to California. Like other chickadee species, it travels in foraging flocks that may suddenly appear and quickly move through an area, sometimes attracting other species such as kinglets, nuthatches, and warblers. The **Winter Wren** is a tiny bird of the understory. Dark reddish brown with a stubby tail, it sings a long, loud, melodious warble from a song perch, usually a branch on a fallen tree. A buzzy trill from high in a conifer might be that of a **Townsend's Warbler.** The adult male has a bright yellow face and breast, punctuated by bold black facial markings.

The **Western Gray Squirrel** is a large, tree-dwelling rodent with a bushy tail. The little **Yellow Pine Chipmunk** is widespread throughout the Pacific Northwest. Not confined to forests, it is often seen in subalpine meadows at high elevations. **Townsend Chipmunk** is larger and darker than the Yellow Pine Chipmunk and is found in deep conifer forest.

The 2-inch **Pacific Treefrog** has a dark line from its nose to its cheek. The **Ensatina** is one of many species of salamanders found in the moist forest undergrowth. When threatened, it will arch its tail and back and may emit a weak squeak. The **Northern Alligator Lizard** is a heavy-bodied, 13-inch lizard found throughout the Pacific Northwest.

Douglas-fir Forest

Range: Throughout the West, but best developed in the Pacific Northwest.

VAUX'S
SWIFT

SPOTTED
OWL

WHITE-WINGED
CROSSBILL

RED
TREE
VOLE

WESTERN
HEMLOCK

NORTHERN
FLYING
SQUIRREL

BIGLEAF
MAPLE

TANOAK

SALAL

COMMON
DOUGLAS-
FIR

HOOKER'S
FAIRY BELL

CALYPSO
ORCHID

PACIFIC
GIANT
SALAMANDER

Common Douglas-fir is found throughout the Rockies, much of the Sierra Nevada, and along the Pacific Coast well into Canada. It reaches its full stature in the Pacific Northwest, attaining heights of over 200 feet and diameters of nearly 8 feet. It is not a true fir; the cones of true firs grow upright, but Douglas-fir cones hang down. The cones have unique three-pointed bracts that project from between the scales. Other conifers such as **Western Hemlock** are found with Douglas-fir.

Tanoak is not a true oak, but it closely resembles one, especially its acornlike fruit. It is evergreen, with thick, leathery, sharp-pointed leaves. **Bigleaf Maple** leaves can measure a full foot in diameter, though young trees usually have smaller leaves. The leaves turn deep yellow-orange in autumn before they drop. **Salal,** with glossy, oval leaves and bell-like flowers, is a common shrub throughout the understory. **Calypso Orchid** and **Hooker's Fairy Bell** are among the many wildflowers in the lush forest.

Douglas-fir Forests are home for the **Spotted Owl,** a bird of deeply wooded canyons and old-growth forests. It is nocturnal, and sits quietly during the daylight hours, often high on a canopy limb. **Vaux's Swift** is commonly seen darting about in forest openings, along rivers, and over the canopy in its aerial search for insects. This small, dark bird flies on slender, stiffly held, rapidly beating wings. The **White-winged Crossbill** pries open cones with its crossed bill to get at the seeds inside.

The **Red Tree Vole** lives its entire life in Douglas-firs, sometimes never leaving the tree of its birth! These voles build large nests up to 150 feet above the forest floor that generations of voles may share, condominium-style. The **Northern Flying Squirrel,** usually out only at night, has huge eyes and wide flaps of skin connecting its forelegs and hindlegs. This skin is used effectively as a parachute when the animal leaps from one tree to the next.

The **Pacific Giant Salamander,** one of the many resident salamanders of moist Pacific Northwest forests, is most easily identified by its large size, much bigger than any other salamander in the region.

Northwestern Riverine Forest 1
(see also page 120)

Range: Southern Alaska through northern California and the Sierra Nevada.

BLACK SWIFT

WILLOW FLYCATCHER

BLACK COTTONWOOD

PACIFIC WILLOW

female

male

BARROW'S GOLDENEYE

SALMONBERRY

fruit

ROUGH-SKINNED NEWT

MONKSHOOD

OLYMPIC SALAMANDER

The rivers of the Pacific Northwest are fed each spring by snowmelt from the mountains, filling waterways with crystal water rich in minerals. The swift rivers are oxygen-rich and generally unpolluted, making them ideal habitats for salmon and trout. The fish in turn attract many birds and mammals.

Black Cottonwood lines rivers throughout the Pacific Northwest. Like all cottonwoods, it is a rapidly growing tree that needs plenty of light. Leaves are always triangular and sharply pointed, but they vary in girth; some are wide, some thinner. The upper side of the leaf is dark, shiny green, while the lower side is silvery. In autumn, the leaves turn golden yellow.

Red Alder is the largest of the alders, attaining heights of up to 130 feet, though 40–60 feet is much more typical. Alders are unusual trees in that they are capable of taking nitrogen gas from the atmosphere and combining it with oxygen into a usable form that adds to soil fertility. **Oregon Ash** has compound leaves divided into 5–7 oval, wavy-edged leaflets. The leaves turn yellow and drop off in autumn. Approximately 30 willow species occur in the Pacific Northwest, including **Pacific Willow.** Leaves are slender, dark shiny green, and distinctly toothed. **Cascara Buckthorn** is often shrubby, but on moist sites it can grow to tree size, up to 40 feet tall. It is essentially an understory species, shade-tolerant and slow-growing. The leaves are deciduous and birch-like, oblong with tiny teeth and parallel veins.

Salmonberry is one of the most abundant shrubs in the Pacific Northwest. It grows along roadsides, in open areas, and along woodland trails, and is particularly common along rivers and streams. The shrub produces large, pinkish red flowers that mature into a blackberry-like, dull red fruit. Many birds feed on the fruits.

Poisonous **Monkshood** is one of the most colorful of the many wildflower species found near rivers and streams. It is easily identified by its uniquely shaped, deep violet flowers on tall stalks. **Yellow Skunk Cabbage** is a member of the arum family, a group widely distributed in the American tropics. The leaves are

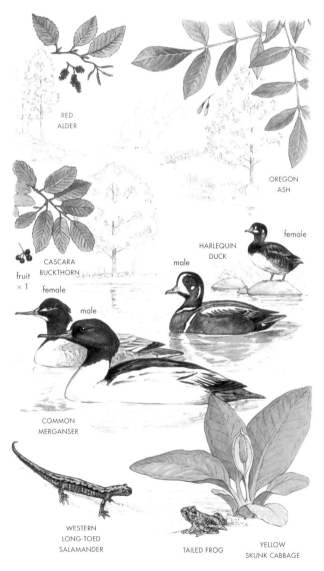

RED
ALDER

OREGON
ASH

CASCARA
BUCKTHORN

fruit
× 1

female

HARLEQUIN
DUCK

female

male

male

male

COMMON
MERGANSER

WESTERN
LONG-TOED
SALAMANDER

TAILED FROG

YELLOW
SKUNK CABBAGE

huge and have a putrid odor that is evident when the leaf is broken.

Several duck species nest along Pacific Northwest rivers. **Barrow's Goldeneyes** pair off in winter and migrate together, eventually to nest in tree cavities near secluded lakes. The abundance of fish in northwestern rivers attract mergansers, sleek diving ducks that have serrated bills capable of holding fish. **Common Merganser** males are mostly white but with dark backs and dark green heads. Females are gray, with chestnut-colored heads. Like goldeneyes, they nest in tree cavities. Colorful **Harlequin Ducks** nest along swift streams and rivers throughout the region, from far northern Alaska south through western Montana and Idaho. They do not nest in tree cavities but on the ground, usually on a gravel bar.

The **Black Swift** is one of the rarer bird species of the region. It has a strong habitat preference for cliffs, especially those with waterfalls spilling over the edge. Look for their characteristic flight pattern: they spread their tails and alternate rapid wing beats with gliding. The **Willow Flycatcher** is one of 10 look-alike flycatcher species that are best identified by voice and habitat. The Willow sings a dry, buzzy, two-note *fitz-bew.*

Moisture-loving amphibians are common along rivers, and many salamander species live in the Northwest. One of the most distinctive is the **Rough-skinned Newt,** which ranges from British Columbia south to California. Almost 8 inches long, its rough, warty skin causes some to confuse it with a lizard. Dark above, this newt is bright yellow or reddish orange below. The **Olympic Salamander** is small, at most 5 inches long, and varies in color from orangy brown to greenish black. It inhabits edges of swift streams in shaded areas, where it hunts for small invertebrates. The **Western Long-toed Salamander** occupies a wide range of habitats from dry areas to wet subalpine meadows. It has a remarkable tolerance for cold, often breeding while ice is still present. The male **Tailed Frog** is unmistakable, as it is the only adult frog with a short, stumpy tail. These frogs inhabit swift-flowing steams.

Subalpine Mixed Conifer Forest

Range: Middle to high elevations from Alaska south to northern California.

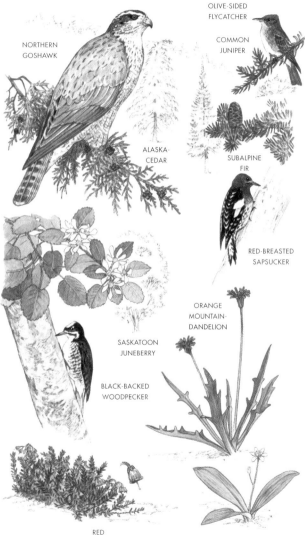

NORTHERN GOSHAWK

OLIVE-SIDED FLYCATCHER

COMMON JUNIPER

ALASKA-CEDAR

SUBALPINE FIR

RED-BREASTED SAPSUCKER

ORANGE MOUNTAIN-DANDELION

SASKATOON JUNEBERRY

BLACK-BACKED WOODPECKER

RED MOUNTAIN-HEATH

BEADLILY

Increasing elevation brings cooler temperatures, more winter snow, increased wind exposure, and a shorter growing season. In this subalpine habitat grow conifers such as **Alaska-cedar, Subalpine Fir,** Mountain Hemlock, and Engelmann Spruce. Each is adapted to withstand the rugged conditions here, though the wind often sculpts them into twisted shapes. High-elevation Subalpine Firs are short and sometimes shrubby, but most retain their symmetrical conical shapes even after being repeatedly burdened with heavy snow. Alaska-cedar has pale, yellowish, scaly foliage that droops in wide sprays. The drooping growth form helps the tree shed snow.

Common Juniper forms dense mats on exposed rocky sites. This evergreen shrub is a conifer with short needles. **Red Mountain-heath,** with delicate pink, bell-like flowers, also forms mats. **Saskatoon Juneberry,** which has clusters of white flowers, is a widely distributed member of the rose family that can be found on mountain slopes from the Rockies through the Southwest and throughout the Pacific Northwest well into Alaska. **Beadlily** is an elegant plant that produces a single, white, six-petaled flower that eventually becomes a pale, shiny blue berry, the "bead." **Orange Mountain-dandelion** is easy to identify, as it is the only orange daisylike flower in the subalpine area.

The **Northern Goshawk**, which occurs in dense forest throughout North America, preys almost exclusively on birds, which it captures with a sudden strike. Goshawks are big predators (up to 26 inches) that tend to feed on larger birds such as grouse and jays. Look for the **Olive-sided Flycatcher** perched high atop a snag on a dead tree overlooking a mountain meadow or alder thicket. Its song is a loudly whistled *HIP-three cheers!* The bird has a characteristic profile, big-headed and upright. The **Black-backed Woodpecker** is often overlooked as it quietly taps on old, burned tree snags that harbor bark beetle larvae. It is the only forest woodpecker with an all-black back. The **Red-breasted Sapsucker** ranges from south coastal Alaska to northern California. It is the only sapsucker with an all-red head and breast.

Northwestern Subalpine Meadows

Range: At treeline and above on mountains throughout the West.

CALLIOPE HUMMINGBIRD

RUFOUS HUMMINGBIRD

YELLOW COLUMBINE

MAGENTA PAINTBRUSH

EXPLORER'S GENTIAN

AVALANCHE LILY

CHIPPING SPARROW

BRACTED LOUSEWORT

WESTERN PASQUEFLOWER

FALSE-HELLEBORE

SPREADING PHLOX

LINCOLN'S SPARROW

When the deep snows of winter finally melt, they leave behind enough moisture to create lush Subalpine Meadows. Over 100 wildflower species grow among a carpet of sedges and grasses during the brief summer growing season. The diversity of color in Subalpine Meadows is stunning: rich **Magenta Paintbrush** scattered among deep lavender **Explorer's Gentian,** punctuated here and there by bright **Yellow Columbine;** dark green mats of pink-flowered **Spreading Phlox** on slopes also covered by scores of bright white **Avalanche Lilies. Bracted Lousewort** advertises for insect pollinators with a dense array of yellow flowers atop a long stalk, often up to 3 feet tall. The leaves look fernlike, and the plant, when not flowering, is sometimes misidentified as a fern. **Western Pasqueflower,** also known simply as "anemone," has densely hairy leaves and stem. Even the flower is a bit hairy, and the seedhead is so hairy that it looks a bit like a little white mouse curled up at the tip of a stalk! The hair may act to help insulate the plant from cold and wind chill.

Several tall plant species thrive in wet subalpine meadows, including **False-hellebore,** or Cornlily, which can attain heights of over 10 feet. This species is considered one of the most poisonous of western plants.

Two hummingbird species frequent the Subalpine Meadows. The **Rufous Hummingbird** is the more common of the two, ranging farther north than any other species. Like virtually all hummingbirds, the Rufous is strongly attracted to the color red. Notice how many tubular flowers are, in fact, red: paintbrushes, penstemons, columbines, monkeyflowers, and beardtongue. The **Calliope Hummingbird** has the distinction of being the smallest of the subalpine birds, even smaller than a Rufous Hummingbird.

The **Chipping Sparrow** ranges very widely over North America, and its repetitive, dry trill can be heard throughout the mountain meadows. **Lincoln's Sparrow,** which has a streaked breast, is attracted to moist habitats such as bogs and wet meadows.

Index